NEW DIRECTIONS FOR STUDENT SERVICES

John H. Schuh, *Iowa State University*
EDITOR-IN-CHIEF

Elizabeth J. Whitt, *University of Iowa*
ASSOCIATE EDITOR

New Challenges for Greek Letter Organizations: Transforming Fraternities and Sororities into Learning Communities

Edward G. Whipple
Bowling Green State University

EDITOR

Number 81, Spring 1998

JOSSEY-BASS PUBLISHERS
San Francisco

New Challenges for Greek Letter Organizations: Transforming
Fraternities and Sororities into Learning Communities
Edward G. Whipple (ed.)
New Directions for Student Services, no. 81
John H. Schuh, Editor-in-Chief
Elizabeth J. Whitt, Associate Editor

Microfilm copies of issues and articles are available in 16mm and 35mm,
as well as microfiche in 105mm, through University Microfilms Inc., 300
North Zeeb Road, Ann Arbor, Michigan 48106–1346.

ISSN 0164-7970   ISBN 0-7879-4213-8

New Directions for Student Services is part of The Jossey-Bass Higher
and Adult Education Series and is published quarterly by Jossey-Bass Inc.,
Publishers, 350 Sansome Street, San Francisco, California 94104–1342.
Periodicals postage paid at San Francisco, California, and at additional
mailing offices. Postmaster: Send address changes to New Directions for
Student Services, Jossey-Bass Inc., Publishers, 350 Sansome Street, San
Francisco, California 94104–1342.

New Directions for Student Services® is indexed in College Student Personnel Abstracts and Contents Pages in Education.

Subscriptions cost $54.00 for individuals and $90.00 for institutions,
agencies, and libraries. See Ordering Information page at end of book.

Editorial correspondence should be sent to the Editor-in-Chief,
John H. Schuh, Campus Box 8, Wichita State University, Wichita, Kansas
67260–0008.

Cover photograph by Wernher Krutein/PHOTOVAULT © 1990.

Jossey-Bass Web address: www.josseybass.com

Manufactured in the United States of America on Lyons Falls Turin Book.
This paper is acid-free and 100 percent totally chlorine-free.

CONTENTS

EDITOR'S NOTES

Greek letter organizations have prospered for many years, largely because of their capacity to unite students in friendship and shared purpose. Being affiliated with a social fraternity or sorority means belonging to a group of "brothers" and "sisters" who care about one another. It creates what former Pennsylvania State University president John Oswald called "an island of smallness on the large ocean that is today's college campus" (Anson and Marchesani, 1991, pp. 1–7).

Nearly 650,000 undergraduates in North America belong to social fraternities and sororities. Greek letter organizations could give these students opportunities for social and cognitive development and could provide their campuses with effective learning environments. Yet research on how college experiences affect student learning raises questions about the educational value of fraternities and sororities. The gap between potential and reality is cause for concern and reflection about the future of Greek letter organizations on campuses.

Purpose and Audience

This volume, *New Challenges for Greek Letter Organizations,* aims to describe and examine critical issues that affect Greek letter organizations today. Higher education in the United States currently faces myriad challenges, including questions about the costs and benefits of higher education, demands for greater accountability to external constituencies, and declining human and fiscal resources. Renewed emphasis on the core functions of higher education—teaching and learning—calls institutions to focus on creating effective learning environments, both inside and outside the classroom. In response, colleges and universities are examining policies, programs, and services to determine their contributions to the institutions' educational mission and to the learning and development of students.

This climate of scrutiny includes social fraternities and sororities. As college and university leaders question the value of Greek membership, the message to Greek letter organizations is clear: if they want to be taken seriously as active partners in students' education, their current practices must change. Although responsibility for accomplishing the necessary change lies with the Greek organizations themselves, senior-level university administrators can facilitate the change process. University leaders can hold the groups accountable to institutional values and policies while supporting their efforts to make important contributions to the campus learning community.

Because of the roles they play in advising student organizations, implementing and enforcing institutional policies and regulations, and overseeing the quality of learning environments outside the classroom, student affairs

1

professionals are key figures in determining the future of fraternities and sororities (Heida, 1990). Indeed, although "the popular press may claim that *in loco parentis* disappeared in the 1960s and 1970s . . . most [senior student affairs officers] would strongly dispute any such notion" (Sandeen, 1991, p. 213). As they work with today's Greek letter organizations, student affairs staff members clearly face challenges in being advocates for both students and increasingly stringent standards of student behavior (National Association of Student Personnel Administrators, 1995; Sandeen, 1991).

Thus, our intended audience is administrators at middle to senior levels on campuses with a Greek system. This includes senior student affairs officers, some of whom may never have belonged to Greek letter organizations or served as Greek affairs advisers. The senior student affairs administrator might have come from the faculty to oversee a student affairs division and may have little experience with the division's multiple roles on campus. The topics addressed in this volume are intended to provide useful information and insights for these and other higher education administrators as they grapple with significant student issues.

Vocabulary and Focus

To present effectively the challenges facing Greek letter organizations today, it is necessary to provide an explanation of certain terms used as well as the focus this volume takes.

Terminology. In this volume, we refer to men's organizations as *fraternities,* women's organizations as *sororities,* and fraternities and sororities together as *Greek letter organizations.* The term *headquarters* denotes the national and international offices of Greek letter organizations, as well as their governing bodies: the National Interfraternity Conference (NIC); the National Pan-Hellenic Council (NPHC), and the National Panhellenic Conference (NPC). When discussing mid-and senior-level student affairs administrators, we refer to *senior student affairs administrators.* This term encompasses a variety of positions (for example, director, dean, or vice president of student affairs) whose supervisory responsibilities include Greek affairs. Finally, we use the phrase *learning community* in several different ways. It refers to the entire institution as a community of learners, as well as to smaller groups on campus that contribute to and support the college or university's educational mission.

Gender Differences. Although the term *Greek letter organizations* encompasses both fraternities and sororities, our use of this language is not intended to discount the differences between college men and women or differences between fraternities and sororities. Research shows that some aspects of Greek experiences affect women and men differently (Kuh and Arnold, 1992; Pike and Askew, 1990; Pascarella and others, 1996). For example, in their study on gender and value differences among Greek members, Testerman, Keim, and Karmos (1994) found that males valued "Conformity (doing what is socially proper, correct and accepted) and Leadership (being in charge of other people, having authority or power over others) more highly than women. . . . Females valued Support (being treated with understanding and consideration, receiving kindness and encouragement from others) and Benevolence (doing things for other people, sharing things with others, being generous) more highly than males" (p. 489). From these and other research results, one could infer that there are differences between sororities and fraternities, and their members, regarding the challenges described in this volume.

Media headlines consistently focus on fraternity men and their problems with alcohol abuse, hazing, and pranks that run the gamut from harmless to life-threatening. This is not to say that women are never involved in similar situations. Sororities, however, tend to have more stringent rules of conduct, including policies about what can or cannot occur in the sorority house. Thus, some of the behavior attributed only to men (that is, binge drinking, loud parties, and hazing) could partly reflect the activity's location—often the fraternity's property or a location rented by the men's group—not the participants.

Another difference between sororities and fraternities is grade point averages. Whereas male Greek grade point averages are lower than those of non-Greek students, female Greek grade point averages are similar to those of non-Greek women (Pike and Askew, 1990). One could infer from this that sororities place a higher value on academic activities and educational goals than fraternities.

In the rest of this volume, we refer to differences between men's and women's groups when they are relevant and supported by research. Issues such as alcohol abuse, hazing, ethics, development of effective learning environments, and chapter standards are not unique to one sex, though. Most of our discussion therefore focuses on Greeks in general.

Racial Differences. We recognize that "since the establishment of a Black fraternity, Alpha Phi Alpha Fraternity, Inc., at Cornell University in 1906, America's institutions of higher learning have struggled with a racially dichotomous Greek system" (Kimbrough, 1997, p. 229). Adding to the struggle is the paucity of research on the nature and impact of historically black Greek organizations (Schuh, Triponey, Heim, and Nishimura, 1992). In general, historically black and predominantly white Greek groups differ in organization, membership, and traditions. These differences are likely to affect the challenges faced by the groups and the institutions in which they reside. Thus, although we intend to provide information that is not exclusive to white Greek organizations, and although we hope the challenges discussed in this volume are of interest to historically black Greek groups, most of the work on which this volume is based relates to predominantly white groups.

New Challenges for Greek Letter Organizations

As colleges and universities renew their commitment to teaching and learning and to developing campus learning communities, it is vital that senior-level administrators understand how Greek organizations figure into this effort. In

Chapter One, Eileen Sullivan and I describe the roles that Greek letter organizations can and should play in a community of learners, as well as the ways in which they fall short as learning communities.

Today, U.S. higher education institutions face the critical challenges of creating diverse learning communities and preparing students to live and work effectively in an increasingly multicultural society. In Chapter Two, Vic Boschini and Carol Thompson discuss the challenge of diversity, including recruiting and retaining members of underrepresented groups and educating fraternity and sorority members about issues of diversity.

Because cognitive development is an essential element of a college education, cocurricular experiences—including Greek membership—that enhance or detract from achieving this purpose merit our attention. In Chapter Three, Kathleen Randall and David Grady probe the challenge of critical thinking, including current research on Greek organizations and cognitive development.

As the value of Greek letter organizations is called into question at institutions of higher education, members must often make difficult choices. In Chapter Four, Cathy Earley examines the ethical dilemmas that require undergraduates to determine the most appropriate course of action.

Student alcohol use is one of the most serious challenges facing higher education in general, and Greek letter organizations in particular. In Chapter Five, Bridget Guernsey Riordan and Robert Dana explore this challenge and offer recommendations.

In Chapter Six, Nicholas Hennessy and Lisa Huson examine the challenge of legal liability. They provide an overview of the legal issues that Greek systems face. Behavior such as hazing, using alcohol, hosting parties, sexually assaulting others, showing negligence, and performing acts of violence could all have legal implications.

In Chapter Seven, Michael Shonrock discusses the high standards that Greeks profess to espouse—and the inconsistent and inappropriate behavior in which they sometimes engage. He explores the challenges raised when the practices in Greek organizations contradict the values articulated in their missions and creeds.

In Chapter Eight, Eileen Sullivan and I revisit the challenges that Greek letter organizations face. We also examine effective strategies that senior student affairs administrators can employ to help Greek letter organizations achieve their potential as learning communities.

We would like to make a final note about the "new challenges" described in this volume. Some readers might wonder whether the challenges we have chosen to address are indeed new. We recognize that alcohol use, campus diversity, legal liabilities, cognitive development, ethical development and standards, and the creation of effective learning environments are not unique to the late 1990s. What is new, however, is the context in which these challenges must be faced. There is clear evidence that this is a critical moment for determining the future of Greek letter organizations. Fraternities and sororities must demonstrate that they can finally face and overcome these challenges and contribute to educational outcomes if they are to survive and thrive. We believe that, to accomplish this, fraternities and sororities must cease to define themselves as *social organizations* and begin to call themselves *learning communities*.

Edward G. Whipple
Editor

References

Anson, J. L., and Marchesani, R. F. (eds.). *Baird's Manual of American College Fraternities.* (20th ed.) Indianapolis, Ind.: Baird's Manual Foundation, 1991.

Heida, D. E. "Greek Affairs in Higher Education: Dilemmas in Philosophy and Practice." *NASPA Journal,* 1990, *28* (1), 3–7.

Kimbrough, W. M. "The Membership Intake Movement of Historically Black Greek-Letter Organizations." *NASPA Journal,* 1997, *34* (3), 229–239.

Kuh, G. D., and Arnold, J. C. *Brotherhood and the Bottle: A Cultural Analysis of the Role of Alcohol in Fraternities.* Bloomington: Center for the Study of the College Fraternity, Indiana University, 1992.

National Association of Student Personnel Administrators. *Reasonable Expectations.* Washington, D.C.: National Association of Student Personnel Administrators, 1995.

Pascarella, E. T., Edison, M., Whitt, E. J., Nora, A., Hagedorn, L. S., and Terenzini, P. T. "Cognitive Effects of Greek Affiliation During the First Year of College." *NASPA Journal,* 1996, *33* (4), 242–259.

Pike, G. R., and Askew, J. W. "The Impact of Fraternity or Sorority Membership on Academic Involvement and Learning Outcomes." *NASPA Journal,* 1990, *28* (1), 13–19.

Sandeen, A. *The Chief Student Affairs Officer: Leader, Manager, Mediator, Educator.* San Francisco: Jossey-Bass, 1991.

Schuh, J. H., Triponey, V. L., Heim, L. L., and Nishimura, K. "Student Involvement in Historically Black Greek Letter Organizations." *NASPA Journal,* 1992, *29* (4), 274–282.

Testerman, M., Keim, M., and Karmos, J. "Values Differences in Greek Affiliation and Gender." *College Student,* 1994, *28* (4), 486–491.

EDWARD G. WHIPPLE *serves as vice president for student affairs and adjunct associate professor in the Department of Higher Education and Student Affairs at Bowling Green State University in Bowling Green, Ohio. He is a former international president of Phi Delta Theta fraternity.*

Today's Greek letter organizations are under greater scrutiny than ever before. Although these groups can contribute to the educational success of their members in important ways, they will not achieve that potential without addressing persistent challenges.

Greek Letter Organizations: Communities of Learners?

Edward G. Whipple, Eileen G. Sullivan

Fraternities and sororities are a uniquely North American phenomenon, existing only in the United States and Canada. Although many much older European universities have a variety of clubs and organizations for students to join, none has anything quite like the modern Greek letter organization.

Since the first institutions of higher education were founded, students have formed groups to feel that they belong and have a community. These groups have taken a variety of forms, from national alliances at the University of Paris to debating societies at Harvard College to the clubs and organizations common in the late twentieth century (Rudolph, 1990). This impetus toward community based on common interests and values led to the development of what we know today as fraternities and sororities.

A Brief History of Greek Organizations

The Phi Beta Kappa honorary fraternity founded in 1776 at the College of William and Mary is the forerunner of today's Greek letter organizations. Phi Beta Kappa established precedents that today's groups still follow, including names composed of Greek letters; secret rituals and symbols that affirm shared values and beliefs; and a badge that, in general, only initiated members wear. Although it can be argued emphatically that today's Greek organizations lack the scholarly emphasis of Phi Beta Kappa, their connections to that society are evident in the outward symbols of fraternity.

Education in early American colleges was rigid at best and oppressive at worst (Johnson, 1972). Curricula were prescribed, and classroom work involved memorization of texts and formulaic disputations. A similar lack of freedom and variety characterized students' lives outside the classroom (Rudolph, 1990). Most students were young men who aspired to be ministers or religious teachers. The lack of intellectual excitement and social freedom in the formal curriculum led these students to form debating societies and literary clubs.

Over time, as the college student population became more heterogeneous and less focused on careers in the Church, many of the debating and literary societies evolved into what we now know as fraternities (Rudolph, 1990). In particular, during the early to mid-1800s, many of these societies developed a much more social focus, primarily because they began to offer housing. Social Greek letter societies began in 1825 with the founding of Kappa Alpha Society at Union College (Robson, 1976).

Fraternities and sororities have always been established to meet specific needs, both cultural and academic, for various campus subcultures. Some groups grew out of specific religious concerns, such as those founded for Jewish or Catholic students. Others grew out of a need for groups similar to those that the majority students already had. When women were admitted to universities, they started their own organizations. Kappa Alpha Theta women's fraternity is credited with starting the Greek letter organization movement for women in 1870 when it established a chapter at DePauw University in Greencastle, Indiana (Jones, 1976).

Throughout their history, fraternities and sororities have faced significant challenges from agencies outside the Greek system, including university administrators, non-Greek students, faculty members, and the general public. Greek organizations have weathered these storms. Today, they are some of the oldest institutions in North America. Their historic ability to change in the face of great challenges shows that they have had the necessary survival skills. This past bodes well for the present.

The Evolving Campus Community

On the college campus today, the term *learning community* describes the environment that many institutions seek to create for their students, faculty, and staff. This effort is the result of a complex set of pressures from inside and outside institutions of higher education. Colleges and universities in the 1990s face serious questions from funding sources and the general public about the costs and benefits of higher education. There are increasing demands for accountability; colleges and universities must demonstrate that higher education does what it says it does (Wingspread Group, 1993). They have responded to these pressures by renewing an emphasis on the core functions of higher education: teaching and learning (American College Personnel Association, 1996; Barr and Tagg, 1995; National Association of State Universities and Land Grant Colleges, 1997). This emphasis is evident in a statement from the Carnegie Foundation for the Advancement of Teaching. In their 1990 report, *Campus Life: In Search of Community,* they say: "What is needed, we believe, is a larger, more integrative vision of community in higher education, one that focuses not on the length of time students spend on campus, but on the quality of the encounter, and relates not only to social activities, but to the classroom, too. The goal as we see it is to clarify both academic and civic standards, and above all, to define with some precision the enduring values that undergird a community of learning" (Boyer, 1990, p. 7).

Institutions have an opportunity to provide multiple learning environments, or communities. The college or university can be viewed as a large learning community composed of several smaller, more varied communities. These communities include classrooms or even small groups within classrooms, such as study groups. Student organizations can also be learning communities. The extent to which these smaller communities complement and contribute to the institution's educational mission will determine its success as a learning community.

Therefore, as institutions attempt to design, develop, and implement the notion of a learning community, all aspects of student life must be examined in light of their contributions to both community and learning. This means that institutions must identify and create environments—both inside and outside the classroom—that most effectively promote learning. Kuh, Douglas, Lund, and Ramin-Gyurnek (1994) have described such environments: "A college or university with an ethos of learning draws in students, compelling them to examine affirming and challenging ideas and perspectives and encouraging them to reflect, ponder, question, debate, and act on their learning. Such institutions value debate, discussion, and the free flow of ideas without regard to topic. They promote programs and avenues through which students may reflect on and make connections between life activities and their larger educational experience, both on and off campus" (p. 61). Successful institutions will develop student-centered, collaborative, and supportive learning communities in which the student's experience shapes knowledge—both in and out of class (Barr and Tagg, 1995).

It is important that institutions expect all programs and services to contribute to an "ethos of learning." For example, students can form learning communities by participating in residence hall activities, belonging to student organizations (such as fraternities and sororities), and being on athletic teams (Schroeder, 1994).

The Student Learning Imperative (American College Personnel Association, 1996), which a group of higher education scholars and administrators developed, offers specific guidelines for student affairs professionals who want to foster student learning and community. The Student Learning Imperative states that student affairs organizations have the opportunity and obligation to create learning communities outside the classroom.

According to Kuh (1996), these professionals must "intentionally create the conditions that foster student learning and personal development" (p. 1), including clear and consistent educational goals, clear and high expectations for student performance, systematic assessment of learning environments, evaluation of policies and programs, extensive opportunities for student involvement, and a pervasive commitment to learning. These "seamless learning environments" (p. 136) are places in which "students must be active, rather than passive, participants in the process and assume a large measure of responsibility for their own learning; faculty and student affairs professionals must focus their time and energy on creating the conditions that foster undergraduate learning; the administration must provide opportunities and resources so that learning can occur; and the institution as a whole must be accountable to its various constituencies" (pp. 144–145).

This ideal calls for a reexamination of program and service philosophy, development, and implementation. Changing student affairs practices in order to build learning communities on a campus requires building coalitions with faculty, students, academicians, parents, and administrators (American College Personnel Association, 1996). The goal is to help all students achieve desired levels of learning and to enhance personal growth and development.

Today's Greek Community

As institutions of higher education try to establish learning communities that are truly "seamless," student affairs administrators must understand students' impact on one another's learning, as well as the influence of student cultures on the development of learning communities. In *What Matters in College,* Alexander Astin summarized his extensive research with these words: "The student's peer group is the single most potent source of influence on growth and development in the undergraduate years" (1993, p. 398). On the college campus, peers convey their impact through frequent interaction, social emphasis, and shared values and attitudes (Dalton and Petrie, 1997; Whitt, 1996). Furthermore, "because peer cultures determine which peers with whom students spend time and from whom they seek approval, these cultures influence the values, attitudes, and beliefs students explore, accept, and reject, as well as the ways in which students direct their attention and energy. . . . Perhaps most important, student cultures influence the extent to which students are integrated into the academic life of the college" (Whitt, 1996, p. 193).

Greek letter organizations constitute a powerful student culture, with powerful implications for their members' learning. If student affairs professionals understand these cultures, colleges and universities are more likely to help students make the peer culture possess values and behaviors that are consistent with the institution's educational priorities (Dalton and Petrie, 1997). In other words, administrators can influence students to create learning communities within the Greek system.

Failure to understand student cultures or to know who the students are can impede any changes that require student support. Indeed, "if the student cultures are not addressed, even the most ambitious elegantly designed institutional renewal strategy will fall short because students themselves determine the social context in which learning occurs" (Kuh, 1996, p. 141).

Although the 1990s have seen Greek membership at an all-time high with 400,000 men and 250,000 women (Kuh and Arnold, 1992), these organizations' place in the academy is no longer taken for granted. Some institutions of higher learning question the Greek experience's value for students and for colleges and universities (Sullivan, 1994). Institutional and public scrutiny of the undergraduate collegiate Greek experience stem from the frequent and visible examples of insensitive, illegal, and sometimes tragic incidents that involve fraternities and sororities. Critics claim that fraternities and sororities are exclusionary, sexist, and racist, and that their existence contradicts the values colleges and universities hope to convey to students (Kuh, Pascarella, and Wechsler, 1996; Maisel, 1990; Rhoads, 1995). In addition, the lack of emphasis on academic matters in chapter programming and the pervasiveness of anti-intellectualism reflected in members' behavior have administrators and faculty evaluating the worth of fraternities and sororities to their campuses.

This concern about whether Greeks are or can be viable members of educational communities is not new. Owen and Owen (1976) stated, "What needs to be determined is the essential, enduring worth of the fraternity. The measure of that worth is not quantity—numbers of chapters and members, rates of growth, corporate holdings—but quality as evidenced in the values, purposes and experiences that strongly affect human lives" (p. 2). Wanting Greek organizations to make positive contributions to members' undergraduate experiences, higher education administrators and faculty are frustrated that this has not come to pass. Although institutions and Greek letter organizations' headquarters have increased education efforts and disciplinary measures, the effects have been negligible.

For example, such activities as hazing and binge drinking still occur too frequently. Alcohol use, intellectual development, and personal development are all affected by membership in a Greek letter organization (Kuh, Pascarella, and Wechsler, 1996; Pascarella and others, 1996; Terenzini, Pascarella, and Blimling, 1996). Research also indicates that Greek affiliation can have a negative impact on students' cognitive development by the time the first year of college ends (Pascarella and others, 1996). These and other examples of research about the impact of Greek membership on college behaviors and performance will be described in detail throughout this volume.

Another perspective on the value of the Greek experience is found in the National Interfraternity Conference and National Panhellenic Conference's 1997 research. This research confirmed what proponents of the undergraduate Greek experience have asserted. Those who join fraternities and sororities in college are more likely to volunteer and to be active in civic affairs during adulthood. This factor is referred to as *social capital,* a term often used as a measure of civic participation. The research also showed that members of Greek letter organizations are more likely to contribute financially to charitable and nonprofit organizations and religious groups, and to do so in greater amounts. In addition, the study found that members of Greek letter organizations are more likely than non-Greek students to be involved in college organizations.

Furthermore, alumni of Greek letter organizations are more satisfied than non-Greeks with their social development during college (Thorsen, 1997).

How do higher education leaders reconcile what appear to be conflicting conclusions? Certainly, both bodies of research look at different kinds of outcomes. They have also been conducted by different researchers with their own agendas. The important point for administrators to keep in mind is that all research evidence must be scrutinized in light of an institution's goals, missions, and desired outcomes. Conflicting findings can obviously coexist. Yet Greek affiliates' contributions to civic affairs do not negate the binge drinking culture present in fraternities and sororities. No amount of community service with local organizations makes up for destruction to property after a weekend party. Nor does any amount of time spent at pledge study tables compensate for declines in cognitive development or low grade point averages. Higher education leaders can and should hold students accountable for their actions by expressing the following philosophy: "All the good deeds do not justify the sins."

In addition, campus administrators should ask questions such as the following: If Greek organizations say they are valuable to the institution, why do chapter behavior problems persist? Why are the grades of pledges and associate members lower than those of students who do not pledge? Why are hazing incidents still occurring in fraternities and sororities, despite all our educational programming on campus? Why does it appear that Greeks drink to excess? Why are fraternity houses in such states of neglect that students do not want to live in them? Why are faculty and staff so critical of Greek letter organizations that they refuse to assist in advising roles? Why won't alumni come near a chapter house? Such questions must be addressed and answered if Greek communities are to evolve into true learning communities that complement and support a larger institutional community of learning.

The inability of Greek letter organizations to align themselves more closely with institutions' educational missions has led faculty and administrators to review Greek systems. These reviews have been conducted at many campuses, including Gettysburg College, Bucknell University, Colby College, Bowdoin College, and Dartmouth College (Anson and Marchesani, 1991). In the late 1980s, Colby College was the first institution to withdraw official recognition of its sororities and fraternities and then to eliminate the Greek system (Heida, 1990).

Is it possible for Greek letter organizations to change? Can each fraternity and sorority chapter become a true learning community that enhances and complements the institution's learning goals? Possibly. The burden, however, rests on Greek leadership and members to evaluate their chapters and make the commitment to change. Greek letter organizations can only become communities of learners if the students themselves want to create such communities. They will need help. College and university administrators can aid in this endeavor by providing organizational, educational, and financial resources, as well as moral support. This volume will provide suggestions as to what this assistance might include.

Challenges Facing Greek Letter Organizations

Greek letter organizations face many challenges today. Fraternities and sororities must resolve these challenges if they are to become learning communities. Senior student affairs staff must also be cognizant of these challenges as they formulate policies and procedures; these regulations should help fraternities and sororities develop their own learning communities and enhance their members' educational experiences.

These challenges are broad in scope and very different from those that founders of national and international Greek letter organizations faced more than two hundred years ago. According to Ackerman (1990), "The goals and traditions of the founding brothers and sisters have served Greek organizations well. But the needs of young adults as they move toward maturity are markedly different today than when nineteenth-century idealists developed the canons of Greek life" (p. 79). *New Challenges for Greek Letter Organizations* highlights the main areas of concern for all those who want to ensure a positive undergraduate Greek experience.

In this volume, we have chosen to address six major challenges that we believe to be the most relevant to the future of Greek letter organizations as learning communities. These six challenges are diversity, development of critical-thinking skills, alcohol abuse, legal liability, ethical development, and fraternity and sorority standards and expectations. The next six chapters probe each challenge in depth, but we now provide an overview of these challenges as they pertain to Greek letter organizations and their roles in learning communities.

Diversity. The extent to which U.S. society is becoming multicultural is well known, and colleges and universities face increasing demands to prepare graduates who can live and work effectively in a multicultural world. Undergraduate Greek leaders assert that the Greek experience helps students appreciate individuals from diverse backgrounds and cultures. However, historically white Greek letter organizations continue to be predominantly white and homogeneous in their members' social and economic background, culture, and ideology (King, 1996). These groups are still criticized on many campuses for sponsoring activities that have racist implications. Date auctions, for example, imply the buying and selling of people and thereby mock the horrors of slave auctions (Goettsch and Hayes, 1990).

In a longitudinal study encompassing 3,300 first-year students enrolled at eighteen four-year institutions of higher education, Pascarella and others (1996) found that undergraduate students who participated in educational activities and programs focusing on diversity displayed a greater openness to diversity than their peers who did not. Members of Greek letter organizations took part in fewer of these educational programs than their non-Greek counterparts, and Greek members' openness to diversity declined during their first year of college.

Development of Critical Thinking. Cognitive outcomes (such as critical thinking, reasoning, and understanding) are among the primary aims of college (Pascarella and Terenzini, 1991). Therefore, Greek letter organizations must consider these outcomes a priority as they try to become learning communities. Recent research (Pascarella and others, 1996) found, however, that Greek affiliation can negatively affect cognitive development in the first year of college. Previous research indicates that effects of the first year might actually increase over time, so the negative impact of Greek affiliation early in a student's career has serious implications for the whole college experience (Pascarella and others, 1996). The researchers wrote that "involvement in fraternities (and, to a lesser extent, in sororities) during this period may seriously detract from time required to become successfully integrated into academic life. Indeed, our findings suggest that student involvement in Greek life during the first year of college has implications for intellectual growth that are so antithetical to higher education's academic mission that the practice of freshman-year rush and first-year new member activities should be reconsidered" (Pascarella and others, 1996, pp. 254–255).

Alcohol Abuse. Although alcohol abuse on college campuses is widespread, a recent study by the Harvard School of Public Health showed that members of Greek letter organizations are more likely to abuse alcohol than their non-Greek peers (Kuh, Pascarella, and Wechsler, 1996). This finding can promote the quick demise of a Greek letter organization or of the entire Greek system. Describing alcohol use in fraternities, Kuh and Arnold (1992) wrote that "the greatest disappointment is that fraternities, and those who choose to support them, have not taken action to address the cultural context of these groups so that the behavior of fraternity members is closer to the goals espoused by the fraternity" (p. 97). Thus, Greek letter organizations' inability not only to prevent but also to address members' abuse of alcohol is a major barrier to creating environments in which learning can take place.

Legal Issues. Colleges and universities with Greek systems face numerous and increasingly worrisome legal concerns. Hazing and alcohol abuse lead the list of problems that can quickly bring legal action to a campus, followed closely by examples of offensive and insensitive behavior. Forty states have antihazing laws, some nearly twenty years old, but hazing continues. To say that higher education leaders are frustrated with this situation is an understatement. "Advocates of greater punishments for hazing say that they are still in the early stages of the battle and that hazing—much of it dangerous—remains common. They say that society continues to blame the victims and doesn't strongly punish the perpetrators" (Gose, 1997, p. A37). If Greek organizations are to become learning communities and contribute to the larger institutional community, they must address legal liability issues, especially alcohol abuse and hazing.

Ethical Development. Another key outcome of college is the development of moral and ethical values and a sense of integrity. These are, in turn, reflected in behavior (Astin, 1993). Studies show that Greek membership influences this development in a negative way through pledge education and various social events. For example, a "Jamaican-me-crazy party" does not show sensitivity to the valued traditions and cultures of another country, nor does it demonstrate appreciation for cultural differences. In such ways, Greek letter organizations promote activities and values that conflict with their institutions' missions (Kuh, Pascarella, and Wechsler, 1996; Marlowe and Auvenshine, 1982; Maisel, 1990; Hughes and Winston, 1987; Rhoads, 1995; Stombler and Martin, 1994).

Baier and Whipple (1990) articulated the dissonance between Greek letter organizations' stated values and current behavior in this way: "Perhaps one reason fraternities have come under so much negative scrutiny is that in addition to the discipline problems, legal liabilities, injuries, and deaths caused by fraternity hazing, sexual assaults, racism, poor scholarship, and alcohol and substance abuse, educators have been unable to find any evidence that fraternities contribute to the positive moral, ethical, and intellectual development of their members. . . . The challenge to student affairs administrators appears to be clear. We must either find ways to redirect the values systems of the fraternities on our campuses or we should commence the process of eliminating this dinosaur from our midst" (p. 53).

Chapter Standards and Expectations. Clear, high standards and expectations for student behavior are an important element of "seamless learning environments" (Kuh, 1996). Thus, high standards and expectations are important if fraternities and sororities are to become learning communities. Historically, Greek letter organizations have had codes of behavior and standards to which members commit at initiation. If these standards were a part of the daily lives of Greek members, the groups could indeed become effective learning communities. Many groups and members have neglected to "live" their standards and expectations, however (Kuh and Arnold, 1992; Kuh, Pascarella, and Wechsler, 1996).

The Greek Letter Organization as a Learning Community

Greek letter organizations were founded on such qualities as justice, honor, truth, loyalty, love of wisdom, brotherly love, and unselfish service (Anson and Marchesani, 1991). If Greek members adhered to such principles, they could make a strong contribution to the larger learning community. Greek organizations offer unique opportunities for creating living-learning communities; they provide strong connections between members, plentiful opportunities for leadership and self-governance, and expectations for community service. What better foundation for student learning?

To promote a learning environment, however, fraternities and sororities must first view themselves as members of a larger learning community and see opportunities for learning in all aspects of the organization. Greek letter groups have important resources in this regard, including strong national or international organizations that offer educational and financial resources and strong ties to local alumni. Of course, alumni can be barriers to change, but many want their chapters to be educationally productive members of the campus community.

The overarching challenge for Greek organizations, as well as for college and university leaders, is to examine these groups and determine whether they do contribute to and support student learning. If Greek organizations implement the ideals that they claim to cherish, they can undertake productive activities that provide viable educational outcomes. It is imperative that these organizations define themselves as contributing members of the educational institution. If they are unable to do so, their relationship with institutions of higher education may soon be forfeited (Ackerman, 1990).

References

Ackerman, R. "The Survival of Greek Life: Concerns and Solutions." *NASPA Journal,* 1990, *28* (1), 78–81.

American College Personnel Association. *The Student Learning Imperative: Implications for Student Affairs.* Washington, D.C.: American College Personnel Association, 1996.

Anson, J. L., and Marchesani, R. F. (eds.). *Baird's Manual of American College Fraternities.* (20th ed.) Indianapolis, Ind.: Baird's Manual Foundation, 1991.

Astin, A. W. *What Matters in College? Four Critical Years Revisited.* San Francisco: Jossey-Bass, 1993.

Baier, J. L., and Whipple, E. G. "Greek Values and Attitudes: A Comparison with Independents." *NASPA Journal,* 1990, *28* (1), 43–53.

Barr, R. B., and Tagg, J. "From Teaching to Learning: A New Paradigm for Undergraduate Education." *Change,* Nov.–Dec. 1995, pp. 13–25.

Boyer, E. *Campus Life: In Search of Community.* Princeton, N.J.: Princeton University Press and Carnegie Foundation for the Advancement of Teaching, 1990.

Dalton, J. C., and Petrie, A. M. "The Power of Peer Culture." *Educational Record,* 1997, *78* (3–4), 18–24.

Goettsch, J. M., and Hayes, M. A. "Racism and Sexism in Greek Events: A Call for Sensitivity." *NASPA Journal,* 1990, *28* (1), 65–70.

Gose, B. "Efforts to End Fraternity Hazing Said to Have Largely Failed: Critics Say State Laws Have Been Ineffective, in Part Because of a Tendency to Blame the Victims." *Chronicle of Higher Education,* Apr. 18, 1997, pp. A37–A38.

Heida, D. E. "Greek Affairs in Higher Education: Dilemmas in Philosophy and Practice." *NASPA Journal,* 1990, *28* (1), 3–7.

Hughes, M., and Winston, R. "Effects of Fraternity Membership on Interpersonal Values." *Journal of College Student Personnel,* 1987, *28* (5), 405–411.

Johnson, C. S. *Fraternities in Our Colleges.* New York: National Fraternity Foundation, 1972.

Jones, B. M. "The American Fraternity . . . A Brief Overview." Speech, 1976.

King, P. M. "The Obligations of Privilege." *About Campus,* 1996, *1* (2), 2–3.

Kuh, G. D. "Guiding Principles for Creating Seamless Learning Environments for Undergraduates." *Journal of College Student Development,* 1996, *37* (2), 135–148.

Kuh, G. D., and Arnold, J. C. *Brotherhood and the Bottle: A Cultural Analysis of the Role of Alcohol in Fraternities.* Bloomington: Center for the Study of the College Fraternity, Indiana University, 1992.

Kuh, G. D., Douglas, K. B., Lund, J. P., and Ramin-Gyurnek, J. *Student Learning Outside the Classroom.* ASHE-ERIC Higher Education Report no. 8. Washington, D.C.: Association for the Study of Higher Education, 1994.

Kuh, G. D., Pascarella, E. T., and Wechsler, H. "The Questionable Value of Fraternities." *Chronicle of Higher Education,* 1996, 43 (4), A68.

Maisel, J. P. "Social Fraternities and Sororities Are Not Conducive to the Educational Process." *NASPA Journal,* 1990, 28 (1), 8–12.

Marlowe, A. E., and Auvenshine, C. D. "Greek Membership: Its Impact on the Moral Development of College Freshmen." *Journal of College Student Personnel,* 1982, 23 (1), 53–57.

National Association of State Universities and Land Grant Colleges. *Returning to Our Roots: The Student Experience.* Washington, D.C.: National Association of State Universities and Land Grant Colleges, 1997.

Owen, K. C., and Owen, S. M. "Toward the Year 2000: Perspectives on the American Fraternity Movement." In T. C. Schreck (ed.), *Fraternity for the Year 2000.* Commission on the American College Fraternity for the Year 2000, American College Fraternity Bicentennial Commission, 1976.

Pascarella, E. T., Edison, M., Whitt, E. J., Nora, A., Hagedorn, L. S., and Terenzini, P. T. "Cognitive Effects of Greek Affiliation During the First Year of College." *NASPA Journal,* 1996, 33 (4), 242–259.

Pascarella, E. T., and Terenzini, P. T. *How College Affects Students: Findings and Insights from Twenty Years of Research.* San Francisco: Jossey-Bass, 1991.

Rhoads, R. A. "Whales Tales, Dog Piles, and Beer Goggles: An Ethnographic Case Study of Fraternity Life." *Anthropology and Education Quarterly,* 1995, 26 (3), 306–323.

Robson, J. "The College Fraternity: Two Hundred Years of Service." In T. C. Schreck (ed.), *Fraternity for the Year 2000.* Commission on the American College Fraternity for the Year 2000, American College Fraternity Bicentennial Commission, 1976.

Rudolph, F. W. *The American College.* Athens: University of Georgia Press, 1990.

Schroeder, C. C. "Designing Learning Communities." In C. C. Schroeder, P. Mable, and Associates, *Realizing the Educational Potential of Residence Halls.* San Francisco: Jossey-Bass, 1994.

Stombler, M., and Martin, P. Y. "Bringing Women In, Keeping Women Down: Fraternity 'Little Sister' Organizations." *Journal of Contemporary Ethnography,* 1994, 23 (2), 150–184.

Sullivan, E. G. "The NIC Chronicles: Some Food for Thought About the National Interfraternity Conference." *AFA Perspectives,* 1994, 22 (8), 11.

Terenzini, P. T., Pascarella, E. T., and Blimling, G. S. "Students' Out-of-Class Experiences and Their Influence on Learning and Cognitive Development: A Literature Review." *Journal of College Student Development,* 1996, 37 (2).

Thorsen, E. *The Impact of Greek Affiliation on College and Life Experiences.* Columbia: Center for the Advancement of Social Research, University of Missouri, 1997.

Whitt, E. J. "Assessing Student Cultures." In M. L. Upcraft and J. H. Schuh (eds.), *Assessment in Student Affairs: A Guide for Practitioners.* San Francisco: Jossey-Bass, 1996.

Wingspread Group. *An American Imperative: Higher Expectations for Higher Education.* Milwaukee, Wis.: Johnson Foundation, 1993.

EDWARD G. WHIPPLE serves as vice president for student affairs and adjunct associate professor in the Department of Higher Education and Student Affairs at Bowling Green State University in Bowling Green, Ohio. He is a former international president of Phi Delta Theta fraternity.

EILEEN G. SULLIVAN is completing her doctoral degree in higher education administration at Bowling Green State University. Prior to attending Bowling Green, she was assistant director of student life for Greek affairs at Eastern Illinois University.

If Greek letter organizations are to be effective learning communities, they must be prepared to meet the challenges associated with recruiting and retaining members of underrepresented populations, as well as educating all members about diversity issues.

The Future of the Greek Experience: Greeks and Diversity

Vic Boschini, Carol Thompson

The college student population has changed dramatically since 1776, when Phi Beta Kappa was founded at the College of William and Mary in Williamsburg, Virginia. Historically white fraternities and sororities were established on predominantly white campuses at a time when the student body was primarily white, Christian, and male. Now, however, the college student population is more diverse than it has ever been (Hodgkinson, 1985; Kuh, 1991). If Greek letter organizations are to survive and flourish within the modern college and university, it is imperative that they understand the importance of diversity.

Campus Demographics Today

Although the meaning of *diversity* varies by region and institution, it is undeniable that student populations are far from homogeneous. Among today's college students, some have disabilities; are of nontraditional age; come from different countries; have different sexual orientations; or have varied religious, ethnic, racial, and socioeconomic backgrounds. Rendón and Hope (1996) predict even more significant changes in student demographics by the year 2012. Distance-learning opportunities, such as classes on the Internet, and an infusion of even larger numbers of adult and part-time learners will further change the composition of the student body, and, therefore, institutions' educational priorities.

Persons of color are a growing percentage of the total United States population. Projections show that "between 1990 and 2030, the population of whites in the United States will increase about 25.0 percent, the black population about 68.0 percent, the Asian American, Pacific Island American and the

American Indian population about 79.0 percent, and the Hispanic population about 187.0 percent" (Manley, 1990, p. 1). Students in higher education—now and in the future—reflect these demographic changes.

The Chronicle of Higher Education Almanac reported the following data on students attending college in 1996: 55.0 percent of undergraduate students were women, 24.6 percent were members of an ethnic or racial minority, and approximately 36.0 percent were above age twenty-two (Chronicle of Higher Education, 1996). With the passage of Section 504 of the Rehabilitation Act of 1973 and the 1990 Americans with Disabilities Act, the number of college students with physical and learning disabilities also increased.

Diversity in the Institution

Much of the research about student diversity has noted that students from previously underrepresented groups feel alienated from the rest of the campus community (Fleming, 1984; Evans, 1985; Smith, 1989; Rendón and Hope, 1996). Many of these students feel that the campus community is hostile rather than welcoming and is unaware of their interests and needs.

There is increasing emphasis on creating campus climates that embrace diversity in its broadest definition (American Council on Education, 1988; Rendón and Hope, 1996; Smith, 1989). At the same time, administrators, faculty, and students are addressing and redefining the meaning of learning community. What is community? What defines a community of learners? What makes a community healthy, vibrant, respectful, compassionate, and engaging? How does a learning community support and provide environments and experiences that value diverse perspectives and abilities? How can the need for shared meanings and purposes be balanced with the need for a multiplicity of experiences and perspectives?

These questions are also relevant to student organizations, including sororities and fraternities. What role do student groups play in creating and sustaining a campus climate that welcomes diversity? How do students influence the campus learning community? What roles do Greek letter organizations play in creating—or inhibiting—a campus climate that appreciates and includes differences? How have sororities and fraternities addressed the range of needs and issues directly affecting the development of a diverse learning community? For example, what prevents students of diverse backgrounds from joining Greek organizations?

Two issues of context have bearing on this discussion: (1) all institutions have a context and (2) Greek letter organizations are private in nature. Both of these contexts affect how people on campuses regard diversity.

The Institutional Context. When attempting to answer the tough questions raised by increasing student—and societal—diversity, one must consider the context of each campus (Kuh, Schuh, Whitt, and Associates, 1991). Higher education institutions in the United States can be public, private, religious, military, historically black, or single-sex. They can specialize in liberal arts or technology. This institutional diversity does not guarantee, however, that a particular institution has as diverse a student body as it might desire. In some cases, the institutional mission might limit student diversity. Other factors include geographic location, physical characteristics of the campus, flexibility of programs and services, and institutional priorities. Thus, to have a so-called diverse learning community means many different things across institutions (Smith, 1989).

An institution is also defined by its culture, including its history, traditions, values, and beliefs (Kuh and Whitt, 1988). Each of these factors then influences the environment and how individuals and groups interact within that environment. Institutional responses to diversity are therefore shaped by cultural factors within the institution.

Student groups, including fraternities and sororities, help shape the institution's character and culture; conversely, those institutional characteristics influence student groups. Students' roles in fostering a positive climate for diversity must be viewed in this larger context.

Has the institution made a commitment to diversity? If so, how has this commitment been communicated and implemented? Has the institution involved students and student organizations in discussing this commitment and its expectations of students in regard to diversity? How do institutional leaders, administrators, and faculty model this commitment? Do the campus community members, programs, and leadership demonstrate respect for diversity? What about the facilities and any artwork on campus?

Students learn from what institutions do, not just from what institutions say (Kuh, Schuh, Whitt, and Associates, 1991). Gaps between what a campus espouses and what it enacts with regard to diversity communicate important lessons to students about inclusion, multiculturalism, and integrity. Students can be expected to act on those lessons.

The Privacy of Organizations. Greek letter organizations are private, voluntary, self-governing entities. Students can select an organization's members, elect their own officers, and administer their own operations. Although fraternity and sorority members have the power to govern themselves, they are still accountable in many ways to alumni, the university, and the Greek governing organizations on campus. Colleges and universities cannot tell fraternities or sororities whom to select as members, but they can provide a vision, culture, and support systems that explicitly and genuinely support diversity.

The Greek Role in Embracing Diversity. Colleges and universities need to embrace diversity and create hospitable and inclusive learning communities. Part of the challenge for institutions is to team with Greek letter organizations in this effort. In the remainder of this chapter, we consider why Greek letter organizations ought to be concerned about diversity. We also offer strategies for helping Greeks face this challenge.

The Importance of Caring

Why should Greek letter organizations care about issues of diversity? First, fraternities and sororities were founded on principles of friendship, scholarship, leadership, rectitude, and service. These are honorable values that provide a strong foundation for any learning community. Many students from underrepresented groups share these values and seek experiences based on them but feel alienated from the general campus community and many student organizations (Madrazo-Peterson and Rodriguez, 1978; Loo and Rolison, 1986). The expansion of fraternity and sorority membership to more students who share the organization's values can enhance the Greek experience for all members.

Second, diverse memberships expand the educational and learning opportunities among and between fraternity and sorority members of different cultures, abilities, and backgrounds. Diversity in organizations helps prepare members for working and living in a highly diverse society. The National Study of Student Learning (Pascarella and others, 1996) found, however, that "Greek affiliation had a significant negative effect on openness to challenge and diversity for both men and women." The researchers speculated that one explanation of these results was the homogeneity of Greek groups. Greek letter organizations must address this problem seriously and quickly. Those that do not will likely find themselves in a position that is incompatible with institutional goals and values. In most cases, these same groups face a loss of institutional support and recognition. Even worse, from an educational perspective, is the hobbling effect of homogeneity.

Third, the traditional-aged white student will become the minority on campuses in the next fifteen years (Rendón and Hope, 1996). To remain healthy and viable, fraternities and sororities must actively seek members from within a diverse student body. The groups that do not expand their membership pool will not survive. At best, these groups will become small organizations with little impact on campus student life.

Fourth, fraternities and sororities espouse values of brotherhood, sisterhood, and community. The Greek community, however, cannot exist apart from, or in opposition to, the college or university community. Policies, mission statements, standards, certain traditions, and goals all define what it means to be a member of a college community; these proposals often include expectations of diversity and inclusion. To continue to be part of the college community, Greek letter organizations must conduct themselves according to these goals.

Thus, it is clear why Greek letter organizations should be concerned about diversity. The learning and success of student members, as well as the survival of Greek organizations and the college community, depend on it.

Strategies for Working with Greeks on Diversity

The job functions and role of the senior student affairs officer have changed dramatically in the past few decades (DeWitt, 1991). Students' demands for the vice president's time have increased as students' lives have become more complex. Many senior student affairs officers indicate that an inordinate amount of their time is spent on damage control for activities and events within fraternity and sorority chapters, especially fraternities (Heida, 1990).

To work effectively with Greeks, senior student affairs officers need to understand the role the Greek community plays—and has played in the past— at their particular campus. The senior student affairs officer, as well as members of the Greek affairs staff, should also be familiar with who their Greek students are. That includes their numbers, backgrounds, academic achievements, community contributions, persistent problems.

Finally, the senior student affairs officer should know about Greek organizations' national and international headquarters and governing body activities. The officer should have a rapport with their personnel. When student affairs officers work with undergraduate chapters on difficult matters, such as promoting openness to diversity, they should view these groups as partners.

Fraternities and sororities face the challenge and opportunity of responding to the changing composition of the undergraduate student body (Bryan and Schwartz, 1983; Winston, Nettles, and Opper, 1987). Not unlike other segments of the university community, such as academic departments and faculty and campus leadership, Greek organizations need to be educated about how student characteristics are changing. They must learn about the importance of creating diverse learning communities. Sororities and fraternities also need to understand the impact of their current programs, practices, and cultures on the campus climate for diversity. Furthermore, they need to understand the individual and organizational advantages they will obtain if students from previously underrepresented groups join their organizations.

Greek letter organizations must go beyond gaining an understanding, however; they need to take action. They must commit to creating diverse learning communities within the Greek system. They should also evaluate and change recruitment, education, and social programs to reflect the interests, needs, and sensitivities of the changing student population.

We offer the following suggestions for senior student affairs officers working with the Greek community and the institution to address the issues of diversity. It is important that Greek letter organizations take responsibility for implementing these strategies. The senior student affairs officer can, however, support these groups. This support can take a variety of forms—fiscal resources, staff involvement, program ideas, and so on. The key for the senior student affairs officer is to work with the Greek letter organizations to help them understand and confront the myriad issues involved in embracing diversity.

1. Make a commitment to diversity—as an institution and as a Greek system. This commitment must be articulated to the entire campus community in many venues so that the expectations are clear. This should be done with integrity, of course. That is, the Greek student leadership must follow through on their commitment and be willingly held accountable for acting or not acting on this stated commitment to diversity.

2. Encourage others to invest in this commitment to diversity by involving key representatives from the Greek system, academic and student affairs, and other students in all educational efforts, assessment processes, and planning activities. The success of any effort depends on how involved interested parties are in understanding and confronting issues, challenges, and opportunities.

3. Assess the institution and the Greek community. The goal of this assessment should be to develop a current and accurate picture of the climate for diversity. This diversity assessment should go beyond gathering and comparing demographic data. It should also assess campus climates; institutional and Greek policies, programs, and practices; and physical environments. The assessment should seek information from faculty, staff, administrators, members of the Greek community, and non-Greek students. A comprehensive assessment should produce a better understanding of activities, behaviors, and attitudes that support, or conflict with, the commitment to diversity. Sample assessment questions can be found in the appendix later in this chapter.

4. Design a plan to address whatever the assessment has identified as needing more attention. This can be done by giving Greek representatives and the university leadership the opportunity to review and discuss the assessment findings jointly; they can identify the emerging issues and themes and develop strategies for improvement. The Greek members who helped design the plan can choose the important messages to be communicated. They should communicate this plan to fraternity and sorority alumni, headquarters, advisory boards, current members of Greek organizations, campus leaders, faculty, and staff. Greek chapters that improve the learning community for students of all backgrounds should be recognized.

5. Inform this process with research on student learning and principles of student development. Everyone has something to learn about what makes a learning community effective, but this is a particularly crucial developmental process for students. Appropriate strategies focused on diversity education should be employed to help students at every level gain a greater appreciation and understanding of diversity issues.

6. Be prepared to allocate adequate resources to build strong and effective educational and support mechanisms. This involves both money and time. Memberships in these student organizations turn over regularly, and efforts to make long-lasting impacts in terms of diversity must not ignore this dynamic.

Concluding Thoughts

One of the biggest challenges for today's senior student affairs officers is to engineer positive and developmental change from within the Greek chapters. At the same time, few tasks are as important as shaping colleges and universities into diverse and effective learning communities. Greek letter organizations play a critical role in the campus climate for diversity. What will help senior student affairs officers in meeting these challenges is to view the activities of Greek letter organizations as providing teachable moments and opportunities for experimentation and growth (Kuh, Schuh, Whitt, and Associates, 1991).

Appendix

The following questions provide a beginning framework for self-assessment by Greek letter organizations and the institution. Each campus should develop its own assessment questions. These questions go beyond simply gathering demographic information about the student body. They illuminate experiences, community and climate issues, student needs, and critical practices that must be looked at comprehensively if the institution and Greek organizations are to address the diversity needs of their campus.

An assessment of the Greek community must be conducted in the context of the institution. Information and data gathered from the institutional perspective, as well as from the Greek perspective, will have more meaning. The data collected from this will allow for a greater understanding of any issues, needs, and themes that emerge. Areas in which the two perspectives concur and conflict will become more evident.

Institutional Self-Assessment

1. Who are your students? (Are they studying at the undergraduate or graduate level? Are they part-time or full-time students? What is their race and ethnicity, sexual orientation, religion, nationality, gender, and age? What disabilities do they have?)
2. What physical barriers exist for students with disabilities?
3. How has the student body changed in the past three to five years?
4. What student needs and issues have emerged?
5. Has a campus climate assessment been done recently? If so, what did it say?
6. What are the institution's recruitment priorities?
7. What are the campus artifacts and traditions? What messages do these campus artifacts and traditions send about the campus community? Do these artifacts and traditions reflect appreciation for a community with diverse students, faculty, and staff?
8. What attitudes do faculty, staff, and students have toward a diverse learning community?
9. What is their commitment to a diverse learning community?
10. How does the administration communicate this commitment?
11. What policies and practices should be reviewed to ensure a commitment to diversity?
12. How are behaviors addressed when they are inconsistent with a diverse learning community?
13. What attitudes do the administration, faculty, and non-Greek students have toward the Greek community?

Greek Self-Assessment

1. What is the current relationship between the Greek community and the institution? How is that relationship defined?
2. Is there a written Greek relationship statement? If so, what does it say?
3. What written and unwritten institutional expectations apply to fraternities and sororities?
4. What kind of educational programming has been provided to the community regarding the changing student body and diversity needs?
5. What institutional support is there for the Greek governing association student leaders and Greek life staff to provide diversity education and other critical services?
6. What is the demographic makeup of the fraternities and sororities?
7. How does the Greek community define diverse membership?
8. What has been done to increase the number of students of different ages, races, religions, ability levels, and nationalities in Greek letter organizations? How successful have these efforts been?
9. What are the barriers to membership for students of diverse backgrounds?
10. Which fraternity and sorority behaviors, traditions, activities, symbols, practices, and values alienate individuals of diverse backgrounds?
11. What kinds of outreach programs have been conducted to educate students from these different backgrounds about the benefits of Greek membership?
12. What are the written and unwritten values of the Greek community?
13. Have policies, practices, and programs been reviewed to reflect a value of openness to diverse memberships?
14. How has inappropriate behavior that reflects insensitivity toward diverse populations been addressed?
15. What attitudes does the Greek community have toward non-Greek students?
16. Are the chapter facilities able to accommodate persons with disabilities?
17. Are programs flexible enough to appeal to students who work, who are of nontraditional age, or who have extensive academic commitments (for example, internships, study-abroad programs, or research fellowships)?
18. How welcoming is the Greek community for individuals whose sexual orientation or ethnic or racial background is not a part of the majority culture?
19. What has the membership experience been like for students of diverse backgrounds who have joined Greek letter organizations?
20. What is working well for these students? What is not supporting their success as individuals?

References

American Council on Education. "Commission on Minority Student Participation in Education and American Life." In *One-Third of a Nation*. Washington, D.C.: American Council on Education, 1988.

Bryan, W. A., and Schwartz, R. A. (eds.). *The Eighties: Challenges for Fraternities and Sorori-ties.* Washington, D.C.: ACPA Media, 1983.

Chronicle of Higher Education. *The Chronicle of Higher Education Almanac.* Chicago: University of Chicago Press, 1996.

DeWitt, R. C. "Managing a Student Affairs Team: It's a Whole New Ballgame." *NASPA Journal,* 1991, *28* (2), 185–188.

Evans, N. J. (ed.). *Facilitating the Development of Women.* New Directions for Student Services, no. 29. San Francisco: Jossey-Bass, 1985.

Fleming, J. *Blacks in College: A Comparative Study of Students' Success in Black and in White Institutions.* San Francisco: Jossey-Bass, 1984.

Heida, D. E. "Greek Affairs in Higher Education: Dilemmas in Philosophy and Practice." *NASPA Journal,* 1990, *28* (1), 3–7.

Hodgkinson, H. *All One System: Demographics of Education, Kindergarten Through Graduate School.* Washington, D.C.: Institute of Educational Leadership, 1985.

Kuh, G. D. "The Demographic Juggernaut." In M. J. Barr and M. L. Upcraft (eds.), *New Futures for Student Affairs.* San Francisco: Jossey-Bass, 1991.

Kuh, G. D., Schuh, J. H., Whitt, E. J., and Associates. *Involving Colleges: Successful Approaches to Fostering Student Learning and Development Outside the Classroom.* San Francisco: Jossey-Bass, 1991.

Kuh, G. D., and Whitt, E. J. *The Invisible Tapestry: Culture in American Colleges and Universities.* Washington, D.C.: Asite Press, 1988.

Loo, C. M., and Rolison, G. "Alienation of Ethnic Minority Students at a Predominantly White University." *Journal of Higher Education,* 1986, *57,* 58–77.

Madrazo-Peterson, R., and Rodriguez, M. "Minority Students' Perceptions of a University Environment." *Journal of College Student Personnel,* 1978, pp. 259–263.

Manley, R. E. "Fraternities' Future Holds Ethnic Diversity." *Fraternal Law,* 1990, *31,* 1.

Pascarella, E. T., Whitt, E. J., Nora, A., Edison, M., Hagedorn, L. S., and Terenzini, P. T. "What Have We Learned from the First Year of the National Study of Student Learning?" *Journal of College Student Development,* 1996, *37* (2), 182–192.

Rendón, L. I., and Hope, R. O. "An Educational System in Crisis." In L. I. Rendón, R. O. Hope, and Associates (eds.), *Educating a New Majority.* San Francisco: Jossey-Bass, 1996.

Smith, D. G. *The Challenge of Diversity: Involvement or Alienation in the Academy?* Report no. 5. Washington, D.C.: School of Education and Human Development, George Washington University, 1989.

Winston, R. B., Jr., Nettles, W. R., III, and Opper, J. H., Jr. (eds.). *Fraternities and Sororities on the Contemporary College Campus.* New Directions for Student Services, no. 40. San Francisco: Jossey-Bass, 1987.

VIC BOSCHINI is vice president for student affairs at Illinois State University. He has served as vice provost for student affairs at Butler University and as a Greek adviser at Western Illinois University.

CAROL THOMPSON serves as associate dean of students at the University of Arizona, where, prior to her current appointment, she served as campus Greek adviser.

Critical thinking is an important outcome of college. Current research in this area pertaining to Greeks is of importance to student affairs administrators who want to create learning communities for and with students.

The Greek Experience and Critical-Thinking Skills

Kathleen Randall, David L. Grady

Interest in the topic of critical thinking can be traced to ancient Greece and Socrates, whose teaching methods are believed to be the first efforts to develop critical thinking (Center for Critical Thinking, 1997). Socrates interacted with students in a way that made them "reflectively question common beliefs and explanations, carefully distinguishing those beliefs that are reasonable and logical from those which—however appealing they may be to our native egocentrism, however much they serve our vested interests, however comfortable or comforting they may be—lack adequate evidence or rational foundation to warrant our belief" (Center for Critical Thinking, 1997). The critical-thinking movement was continued by such writers and thinkers as Aristotle, Thomas Aquinas, Thomas More, Isaac Newton, Charles Darwin, and John Dewey (Center for Critical Thinking, 1997).

The American colleges that fostered the early Greek letter organizations encouraged "students to think for themselves beyond the bounds of academic conventionality" (Owen, 1991, p. 1–2). Accordingly, fraternity life on those campuses—which included Union College, the University of Virginia, and Miami University—focused on "orations, debates, the reading of original poems as well as scientific and scholarly papers" (Owen, 1991, pp. 1–2), though not to the exclusion of friendship and fun.

The term *social fraternity* was originally used to describe the social or personal development that members experienced during their college years (Owen, 1991). Over time, however, Greek letter organizations' emphases have shifted so that most people believe that *social* refers to events such as parties, date functions, and even intramurals sponsored by the organizations. They see

NEW DIRECTIONS FOR STUDENT SERVICES, no. 81, Spring 1998 © Jossey-Bass Publishers

these as Greek organizations' primary activities, not the personal development of members.

Critical thinking is central to the mission of American higher education. Colleges and universities want their graduates to think critically—that is, to make judgments based on evidence, reason, and clearly articulated values (Kurfiss, 1988). As institutions of higher education are called to demonstrate that they produce stellar educational outcomes, they are evaluating their programs and services to ensure that these help students achieve institutional educational goals. Among these programs are Greek letter organizations. Therefore, fraternities and sororities also face questions about what outcomes they promote through their chapter goals and programs.

This scrutiny leads us to ask the following questions, which the rest of this chapter will address: Should critical thinking be an outcome of membership in a Greek letter organization? If so, what role should Greek letter organizations play in this development, particularly in the first year of affiliation? As senior student affairs officers help Greek organizations build learning communities, what role should the development of critical thinking play in this effort?

Critical Thinking Defined

As we have stated, many of history's greatest thinkers have reflected upon the nature of critical thinking and ways to develop it. Therefore, numerous definitions of critical thinking exist. For the purposes of this chapter, we use the following definition developed by Scriven and Paul (1996): "Critical thinking can be seen as having two components: 1) a set of skills to process and generate information and beliefs, and 2) the habit, based on intellectual commitment, of using those skills to guide behavior. It is thus to be contrasted with: 1) the mere acquisition and retention of information alone (because it involves a particular way in which information is sought and treated), 2) the mere possession of a set of skills (because it involves the continual use of them), and 3) the mere use of those skills (as an exercise) without the acceptance of their results."

Critical thinking depends on the thinker's motivation. "When grounded in selfish motives, it is often manifested in the skillful manipulation of ideas in service to one's own, or one's group's, vested interest . . . [but] when grounded in fair-mindedness and intellectual integrity, it is typically of a higher order intellectually, though subject to the charge of 'idealism' by those habituated to its selfish use" (Scriven and Paul, 1996).

Critical-Thinking Skills and Their Impact on Student Development

One of the best-known theories about how college students develop critical thinking is William Perry's concept of intellectual and ethical development. According to Perry (1970), intellectual growth occurs in stages, "from a simplistic, categorical view of the world to a more relativistic, committed view. They move from an unquestioning, dualistic framework (right-wrong, good-bad, beautiful-ugly) to the realization of the contingent nature of knowledge, values, and truth. As students move through these stages, they integrate their intellect with their identity, resulting in a better understanding of the world" (Upcraft, Gardner, and Associates, 1989, p. 43).

Clearly, undergraduate experiences contribute to the development of critical-thinking skills. In their widely acclaimed book *How College Affects Students,* Pascarella and Terenzini (1991) estimated that by the time freshmen reach senior year, they have improved their critical-thinking ability by 34 percent. They stated, "College appears to enhance one's ability to weigh evidence, to determine the validity of data-based generalizations or conclusions, and to distinguish between strong and weak argument. There is less support for the claim that college has a unique effect on one's ability to discriminate the truth or falsity of inferences, recognize assumptions, or determine whether stated conclusions follow from information provided" (p. 156).

Critical thinking develops as a result of various college experiences. Many colleges and universities attempt to equip students with these skills through selected courses. Some of these courses, however, teach skills but do not challenge thinking patterns. Thus, critical thinking is often reduced to a mere sequential process of learning how various arguments may be organized (Astin, 1993). Pedagogical approaches that require active student engagement, such as essay exams and classroom debates, are all considered to be effective in challenging students to think outside of the conventional paradigm of learning (Pascarella and Terenzini, 1991).

Yet critical-thinking ability does not develop merely as a result of pedagogical technique or in-class activities. For example, a recent study (Whitt and others, 1997) found that some kinds of out-of-class interactions with classmates were associated with cognitive gains in college. These beneficial interactions might be conversations about ideas presented in class; group studying; discussions about art and music; and discussions with peers who are very different from oneself about politics, religion, and life. Peer interactions were particularly significant in the first year of college (Whitt and others, 1997). In general, "The evidence is clear [that] when peer interactions involve educational or intellectual activities or topics, the effects are almost always beneficial to students" (Terenzini, Pascarella, and Blimling, 1996, p. 156).

Perhaps most important for cognitive development in college is active student involvement, including opportunities to apply what has been learned inside the classroom in real-life endeavors outside of class (Kuh, Douglas, Lund, and Ramin-Gyurnek, 1994; Terenzini, Pascarella, and Blimling, 1996). As Baron and Sternberg (1987) indicated in *Teaching Thinking Skills: Theory and Practice,* "Unless students can learn to think flexibly, look for opportunities to transfer their skills, seek analogies between past and future situations, and transfer their skills [development] is most unlikely to ensue. . . . Students apply principles of thought to their everyday lives because they are given examples of how these principles apply in such situations" (p. 258). Out-of-class activities that have the potential to contribute to gains in critical thinking include discussions about racial issues, attendance at a sexual harassment awareness workshop, and involvement in student clubs and organizations (Pascarella, Whitt, and others, 1996).

It is imperative to consider students' development of critical thinking in terms of the total campus environment. Because in-class and out-of-class experiences and settings contribute to learning and cognitive development (Terenzini, Pascarella, and Blimling, 1996), they must be considered as administrators work with students and faculty to establish a community of learners. As we have seen, the research results also underscore the importance of peers (especially peers of diverse beliefs, attitudes, and backgrounds) in developing critical thinking.

All of this evidence indicates that Greek letter organizations have the potential to foster critical thinking in their members. Research also raises questions, however, about the extent to which this potential has been fulfilled. We turn to this topic next.

The Freshman Year and Greek Affiliation

Few studies have looked at the relationship between Greek affiliation and cognitive development (Pascarella, Edison, and others, 1996). Therefore, researchers in the National Study of Student Learning sought "to assess the unique (or net) effects of Greek affiliation on standardized measures of reading comprehension, mathematics, critical thinking, and a composite measure of cognitive achievement" (pp. 244–245). The study found that with controls applied for precollege cognitive ability, Greek men scored significantly lower than non-Greek men at the end of the first year of college on all four cognitive outcomes. Greek women also tested lower than non-Greek women, but the differences were only significant on reading comprehension and composite cognitive achievement. Further examination of the results for fraternity members indicated that the negative effects were present only for white men; fraternity membership was associated with significant cognitive *gains* for African American men.

The researchers concluded that Greek membership during the first year of college has a negative impact on cognitive development, especially for men and especially regarding critical thinking. The negative impact of Greek affiliation in the first year warrants particular concern. "The first year of college is a particularly important time in the lives of students. It is in the first year that students face tasks of adjustment to the academic demands of postsecondary education, cultivate effective study habits and time management, and further develop assumptions about and expectations for their educational experiences in college. Involvement in fraternities (and to a lesser extent, in sororities) during this period may seriously detract from time required to become successfully integrated into academic life" (Pascarella, Edison, and others, 1996, p. 254).

Other research cited by the same authors demonstrates that trends begun at the end of the first year of college are likely to persist during subsequent years. That is, the disadvantage of fraternity membership could accumulate over the student's time in college (Pascarella, Edison, and others, 1996). This conclusion alone should cause higher education leaders to question seriously the value of fraternities and sororities in the student experience.

We noted earlier that Greek letter organizations could provide important environments that enhance the development of critical-thinking skills and student learning. Why, then, do Greek letter organizations inhibit the development of critical-thinking skills? Many colleges and universities would respond that Greek organizations do not share the institution's educational values and do not understand (or care about) its educational mission and priorities.

Researchers who have studied college students offer possible explanations. The researchers in the National Study of Student Learning speculated that the demands of Greek membership take time away from activities that promote cognitive development. Note that time is not the only concern here; equally important is how that time is spent. As we have said, when students undertake activities that allow them to apply what they have learned in the classroom, they develop critical thinking.

Others have noted that "common to the out-of-class influences that appear to depress or impede student learning (e.g., living at home, working off campus, being a member of a Greek society) is their potential to isolate students from encounters with new ideas and different people" (Terenzini, Pascarella, and Blimling, 1996, p. 158). Given that Greek letter organizations tend to be homogeneous in their membership, they inhibit the "encounters with new ideas and different people" that help people develop critical thinking.

Strategies for Success

How can Greek membership—especially during the first year of college—have positive rather than negative effects on critical thinking? Efforts in this direction must come from the Greek organizations, including headquarters staff and alumni. They will not be successful, though, without institutional guidance, direction, and support. We offer the following strategies for Greek organizations and student affairs officers who want to help Greek members develop critical thinking:

Strategies for Greek Letter Organizations

1. Provide new member education programs that develop problem-solving skills, and have members apply them to chapter experiences. An example of one such effort is challenging students to think about the fraternity's history. (They might ask, for example, What were the founders, who were approximately the same age as we are, experiencing when they wrote the ritual and developed the symbols? What did they hope future members would learn from the ritual?) This would be preferable to the mere memorization and

recitation of the fraternity's history. New member programs should also ask students to reflect on the educational goals of colleges in general and on their own reasons for being in college.

2. Sponsor chapter programs that challenge analytical abilities and welcome diverse opinions. Greek organizations could invite faculty members to dinner to discuss literature from a global perspective, attend fine arts programs and provide a subsequent discussion of the performance or exhibit, and support a program that honestly discusses substance or alcohol abuse among college students.

3. Plan interactive, "hands-on" philanthropy projects that link the chapter with organizations and groups that chapter members would not usually have the opportunity to meet. Rather than just having the student do the assigned project, every philanthropy project should include a opportunity for the student participants to reflect on their experience. Research has shown that reflection increases reasoning abilities, problem-solving skills, and a sense of empowerment (Iozzi, 1990; Hubbard, 1996).

4. Offer career programs reinforcing the concept that our global society requires effective analytical skills, as well as the ability to respond to a wide variety of populations and perspectives in the workplace.

5. Create an open chapter climate in which issues and chapter decisions are discussed openly and all divergent opinions are welcomed. Chapter members should have the opportunity to grasp the fundamentals of critical-thinking procedures and apply problem-solving skills to chapter situations. Provide training in organizational management and decision making that guards against the pressure to conform to the apparent consensus. New members should be included in chapter discussions and operations from the beginning.

6. Encourage Greek letter organization headquarters to develop resources that help to build thinking skills as a component of leadership development.

7. Within the fraternity's organization, undergraduates should make as many day-to-day decisions as possible in order to develop problem-solving skills. This form of decision making may result in a fundamental change in the structure of national and international organizations as alumni, regional advisers, and so on make fewer decisions for the organization.

Strategies for Student Affairs Professionals and Faculty
1. Encourage and welcome the students' and organization advisers' critical analysis of the administration's vision for the campus climate. Inviting students, advisers, headquarters, and alumni to confront campus assumptions and traditions creates a climate that models the importance of critical thinking for the college community.

2. Emphasize to the Greek letter organizations their founding principles, which underscore the support of academic achievement and intellectual development. Work with chapter members to question the purpose of Greek letter organizations and their traditions, programs, and practices. Encourage dis-

cussion about the role Greek organizations play (and can or should play) within the larger learning community.

3. Encourage curricular experiences that have students engage with ideas and apply in-class learning outside of class. Of particular benefit are classes that provide an orientation to campus life, an orientation to the academic goals and traditions of higher education, discussions about shared reading and written work, and development of study and leadership skills (Upcraft, Gardner, and Associates, 1989).

4. Redesign the student affairs division mission to supplement and support academic affairs and to recognize and value the critical-thinking opportunities in out-of-class experiences. When planning programs and activities, include opportunities for participants to reflect upon their experiences to broaden their thinking and perspective.

5. Conduct additional research to determine the impact of the Greek experience on first-year students' cognitive development. In addition, longitudinal studies on Greek and non-Greek students should be conducted to determine the impact of the Greek experience.

6. Consider moving membership recruitment from early fall to mid-fall or spring or to the sophomore year. Pascarella, Edison, and others (1996) found that student involvement in Greek organizations during the first year of college has such negative ramifications for cognitive growth that the custom of first-year rush and first-year member activities should be reexamined. With deferred pledging, students can adjust to the rigors of college without the demands of membership in a Greek organization. Student affairs practitioners should be prepared to aid in such a transition. Of particular concern are the significant fiscal adjustments that chapters must make, particularly during the first year of such a change.

7. Provide chapter officers with resources and development opportunities (for example, workshops and seminars) to help them learn how to support the building of critical-thinking skills within their organizations.

8. Help chapters or the Greek system as a whole develop programs and other opportunities that require students "to encounter a variety of viewpoints in a nonthreatening classroom environment, experience higher level learning, take the perspective of others, examine the consequences and implications of one's decisions, defend one's position, evaluate the range of possible alternatives, consider and recognize the role of self in society, and reflect on one's own value system" (Iozzi, 1990, p. 389). These opportunities could be instituted in new member programs and then enhanced in membership development programs.

9. Provide opportunities for Greek letter organization chapter advisers to meet faculty sponsors of other student organizations and groups, rather than simply the alumni advisers of other Greek organizations. This interaction will broaden the perspectives of both Greek and non-Greek advisers.

10. Provide staff development and faculty outreach programs that highlight the original founding purposes of Greek organizations. Challenge the widely held assumption that Greek life is necessarily anti-intellectual.

11. Emphasize citizenship within the learning community through meaningful faculty-student interaction and educationally purposeful interaction with students outside the Greek system.

Concluding Thoughts

Since 1776, Greek letter organizations have played an important role in the lives of hundreds of thousands of college students. If Greek organizations are to continue to flourish, they will have to remain relevant to institutions' educational goals. One way to ensure that relevance is to recapture the original meaning of "social" Greek letter organizations as groups that are concerned about the personal development of their members. By reclaiming this important role, fraternities and sororities can ensure their relevance to learning communities and to students.

Greek organizations can support the development and enhancement of critical-thinking skills. The success of this endeavor will contribute significantly to Greek members' becoming an integral part of the institution's learning community. If students begin to develop critical-thinking skills that allow them to make connections among all life experiences, they will become better scholars and stronger members of the fraternity or sorority chapter, and thus valuable contributors to the institutional learning community.

References

Astin, A. W. *What Matters in College? Four Critical Years Revisited.* San Francisco: Jossey-Bass, 1993.

Baron, J. B., and Sternberg, R. J. *Teaching Thinking Skills: Theory and Practice.* New York: Freeman, 1987.

Center for Critical Thinking. "A Brief History of the Idea of Critical Thinking." Sonoma, Calif.: Center for Critical Thinking. Created 1996. http://www.sonoma.edu/cthink/University/univlibrary/cthistory.nclk. Accessed Mar. 10, 1997.

Hubbard, S. M. "Increasing Empowerment Through Reflection in Service Learning Programs." Unpublished master's thesis, Graduate College, University of Iowa, 1996.

Iozzi, L. A. "Moral Decision Making in a Scientific Era." In J. C. Kendall and Associates (eds.), *Combining Service and Learning: A Resource Book for Community and Public Service.* Vol. 1. Raleigh, N.C.: National Society for Internships and Experiential Education, 1990.

Kuh, G. D., Douglas, K. B., Lund, J. P., and Ramin-Gyurnek, J. *Student Learning Outside the Classroom.* ASHE-ERIC Higher Education Report no. 8. Washington, D.C.: Association for the Study of Higher Education, 1994.

Kurfiss, J. G. *Critical Thinking: Theory, Research, Practice and Possibilities.* ASHE-ERIC Higher Education Report no. 2. Washington, D.C.: Association for the Study of Higher Education, 1988.

Owen, K. C. "Reflections on the College Fraternity and Its Changing Nature." In J. L. Anson and R. F. Marchesani (eds.), *Baird's Manual of American College Fraternities.* (20th ed.) Indianapolis, Ind.: Baird's Manual Foundation, 1991.

Pascarella, E. T., Edison, M., Whitt, E. J., Nora, A., Hagedorn, L. S., and Terenzini, P. T. "Cognitive Effects of Greek Affiliation During the First Year of College." *NASPA Journal,* 1996, *33* (4), 242–259.

Pascarella, E. T., and Terenzini, P. T. *How College Affects Students: Findings and Insights from Twenty Years of Research*. San Francisco: Jossey-Bass, 1991.

Pascarella, E. T., Whitt, E. J., Nora, A., Edison, M., Hagedorn, L. S., and Terenzini, P. T. "What Have We Learned from the First Year of the National Study of Student Learning?" *Journal of College Student Development*, 1996, 37 (2), 182–192.

Perry, W. G. *Forms of Intellectual and Ethical Development in the College Years*. Austin, Tex.: Holt, Rinehart and Winston, 1970.

Scriven, M., and Paul, R. "Defining Critical Thinking." Sonoma, Calif.: Center for Critical Thinking. Created 1996. http://loki.sonoma.edu/cthink/FResources/Faculty/Defining.html. Accessed Jan. 13, 1997.

Terenzini, P. T., Pascarella, E. T., and Blimling, G. S. "Students' Out-of-Class Experiences and Their Influence on Learning and Cognitive Development: A Literature Review." *Journal of College Student Development*, 1996, 37 (2), 149–162.

Upcraft, M. L., Gardner, J. N., and Associates. *The Freshman Year Experience: Helping Students Survive and Succeed in College*. San Francisco: Jossey-Bass, 1989.

Whitt, E. J., Edison, M. I., Pascarella, E. T., Nora, A., and Terenzini, P. T. "Interactions with Peers and Objective and Self-Reported Cognitive Outcomes Across Three Years of College." Paper presented at the annual meeting of the Association for the Study of Higher Education, Albuquerque, N.Mex., 1997.

KATHLEEN RANDALL is assistant vice president for student affairs, director of student life, and adjunct associate professor in the Department of Administration and Educational Leadership at the University of Alabama–Tuscaloosa.

DAVID L. GRADY is director of the Office of Campus Programs and Student Activities and adjunct assistant professor in the Department of Counselor Education/Student Development Program at the University of Iowa.

Greek letter organizations can and should be vehicles for their
members' ethical development. If fraternities and sororities examine
the ethical challenges they face, they can enhance their contribution to
the campus learning community.

Influencing Ethical Development in Greek Letter Organizations

Cathy Earley

Fraternity and sorority principles proclaim a duty to shape men and women into responsible adults, model citizens, and ethical leaders. Josephson (1992) defines ethics as "the standards of conduct which indicate how one should behave based on moral duties arising from principles of right and wrong" (pp. 19–20). Moral duties oblige individuals to be honest, fair, and accountable, as well as to avoid harming others or treating them with disrespect. College and university learning communities strive to facilitate this kind of ethical development (Pascarella and Terenzini, 1991).

Greek letter organizations were founded to complement and reinforce the institution's highest ideals. Unfortunately, fraternities and sororities meet both the Greek and institutional goals too infrequently (Maisel, 1990). Negative behaviors including abusing alcohol (Wechsler, Kuh, and Davenport, 1996), hazing (Shaw and Morgan, 1990), demonstrating racism and sexism (Maisel, 1990; Rhoads, 1995; Stombler and Martin, 1994), cheating (McCabe and Bowers, 1996), and performing poorly in classes (Maisel, 1990) elicit increasing criticism of Greek letter organizations for not adhering to the values of higher education or to their own founding principles. Although there are some upstanding chapters and upstanding members who make sound ethical judgments, all are tainted by the low standards of their peers.

The founding principles of fraternities and sororities provide an ideal framework for positive ethical development. Terms such as *moral advancement, integrity, truth, goodness, social responsibility, sacred trust,* and *honor* permeate fraternity and sorority creeds, mottoes, and purpose statements. These principles are consistent with moral duties, and a commitment to moral duties fosters ethical decision making (Josephson, 1992). The Greek learning community's development is hampered when fraternity and sorority members do not make their decision making and behavior agree with stated ethical principles.

Greek organizations must evaluate their roles on campus with regard to their members' ethical development and, therefore, with regard to the development of fraternities and sororities as learning communities. This chapter describes the role fraternities and sororities must play in fostering members' ethical development, and it proposes a role for student affairs administrators in encouraging that development.

Ethical Development in Greek Letter Organizations

Models of ethical development (Kohlberg and Kramer, 1969; Chickering, 1969; Perry, 1981; Rest, 1986) offer ways to evaluate how well students develop ethical thinking in Greek letter organizations. We use Rest's theory of moral development here because it "emphasizes several processes involved in the production of moral behavior" (1986, p. 92). These processes are "1) interpreting the situation in terms of how people's welfare is affected by possible actions of the subject; 2) deciding what the ideally moral course of action would be; 3) deciding what one actually intends to do; and 4) executing and implementing what one intends to do" (p. 93). Examining the Greek experience in light of these four processes can help us identify shortcomings in ethical development in Greek letter organizations.

Considering the Consequences of Actions. Before taking action, one should imagine alternative courses of action and identify the consequences that each action would have for others. This process includes considering that other people's welfare could be at stake and recognizing how possible courses of action affect all parties involved.

It is easier to examine possible actions in light of consequences for others when one is in a community that allows members to care about others and to see connections to other people (Willimon and Naylor, 1995). Rest (1986) saw this connection to other people and communities as the mechanism that allows students to begin understanding the moral implications of their actions.

Because "the Greek system provides one of the few places . . . where students can be together in face-to-face, intimate, sustained ways" (Willimon and Naylor, 1995, p. 149), Greek letter organizations can be ideal settings for examining the moral implications of behavior. Members can, for example, consider possible courses of action and the moral implications of those actions in light of commitments to their brothers or sisters and their organization. At the same, however, these intimate communities of peers can form cultures in which pressure to conform elicits behavior that is antithetical to moral action (Kuh and Whitt, 1988), a topic to which we return in the following section.

Thus, it is advantageous that fraternity and sorority members interact with faculty, live in the residence halls or in surrounding neighborhoods, join other campus organizations, participate in the campus student government, and volunteer in the local area with charitable and civic organizations. For example, the American Council on Education's 1996 freshman survey (Astin, 1996) indicated that those likely to join fraternities are also more likely to have been involved in clubs and to have done volunteer work. These are positive indicators that fraternity and sorority members are involved in communities outside their Greek organizations. By interacting with people from various communities, Greek members can recognize their impact on others. In this way, fraternities and sororities can foster commitment to other causes, people, and communities.

Some institutions and Greek letter organizations now use service learning as a powerful vehicle for ethical development. *Service learning* is "a method and philosophy of experimental learning through which participants in community service meet community needs while developing their abilities for critical thinking and group problem-solving, their commitments and values, and the skills they need for effective citizenship" (Cousins, 1994, p. 1). Service learning can enhance ethical development because it includes two critical pieces: *reflection,* which offers a structured environment designed to foster critical thinking, analyzing, meditating, and reasoning; and *reciprocity,* an assumption that both those serving and those being served give, receive, learn, and develop collaboratively (Cousins, 1994). Service learning can allow students to understand how certain actions affect others' welfare; it also enriches the community and helps students learn important social values, such as service and citizenship.

Through a grant from the W. K. Kellogg Foundation, the National Interfraternity Conference implemented the *Adopt-a-School* program to encourage ongoing community service efforts among fraternity and sorority members (Wilbur, 1997). The goal of *Adopt-a-School* is to partner Greek members with elementary school children to improve children's self-esteem, academic performance, and attendance. Almost two hundred college campuses have participated in the program and developed partnerships with local elementary schools since its inception in 1991. Research on this project demonstrated the positive impact of *Adopt-a-School* in the lives of the elementary school children and Greek volunteers. The data indicated that the college volunteers developed a commitment to be more active in their communities. Efforts such as *Adopt-a-School* offer students opportunities to put into practice stated principles of service and citizenship. This helps them appreciate how their actions affect other communities, and it integrates those principles into their daily lives.

Identifying a Moral Course of Action. To understand how Greek letter organizations determine an ethical course of action, we must examine the organizational culture of fraternity and sorority chapters.

Student cultures, including Greek organizations, develop norms by which members are expected to live (Kuh and Whitt, 1988). "Norms define acceptable ways of doing things. . . . We communicate norms through the language we use, the behavior we model, and the criticism we aim at those who do not follow the 'appropriate' norms" (Cherrey, 1990, p. 61). These norms are so pervasive that they come to define the organization and shape members' values.

If group norms do not honor the organization's stated principles, members do not learn to value and integrate those principles into their lives. Unfortunately, in too many cases, the norms that direct Greek members' lives do not reflect such principles as honor, integrity, respect, and truth. For example, a pledge member who questions the purpose of initiation week activities is likely to be viewed as a threat to group norms rather than as an individual courageous enough to question the activity's validity or ethics.

To influence this second component of moral development, senior student affairs officers should acknowledge the powerful and influential norms that exist within the campus Greek community. Educational efforts that focus on changing individual behaviors or that rely on one individual to change a chapter's norms are likely to be ineffective. Furthermore, rules that have been enacted in the last fifteen years to limit or eliminate hazing, the underage consumption of alcohol, students' access to social functions, and the use of kegs (Fraternity Insurance Purchasing Group, 1996) have not adequately changed the norms within many Greek letter organizations. Problems still exist and, for that, chapter leadership must be held accountable. Obviously, if current rules are not working, different approaches must be sought to resolve the problems.

Students must be educated and supported in efforts to question and change norms that violate the educational values of institutions and Greek letter organizations. Administrators, advisers, and alumni involved with fraternities and sororities can influence this process by engaging students in healthy debate about how specific norms support their organizational principles. Discussion of important principles forces students to examine their choices. This, in turn, can help foster their ethical development.

Initiatives such as the *Our Chapter, Our Choice* peer education program, which helps Greek chapters assess unhealthy norms and develop new goals based on fraternal or sororal principles (Linkenbach, 1992), could be used on an ongoing basis. Through a research process designed to evaluate the effectiveness of *Our Chapter, Our Choice,* the Center for the Advancement of Public Health (1996) found that fraternity and sorority chapters that used *Our Chapter, Our Choice* believed that they learned policies, clarified organizational needs, increased awareness of risk management issues, and made changes in alcohol use at social functions (by limiting or removing the alcohol).

In addition, fraternity and sorority members must be expected to know and follow rules. These rules may cover areas such as expectations for behavior, financial responsibility, and participation in campus activities. These kinds of rules are equated with moral action. Rule enforcement can be viewed as a way to implement the second step of moral action that Rest (1986) identified. It is essential, however, that rules for student conduct explicitly convey the institution's educational values (Dalton and Petrie, 1997). When students fail to comply with these rules, the institution and headquarters should intervene. Such intervention not only models to fraternity and sorority members what moral action should have been performed but also ensures that the moral action is actually undertaken.

Selecting a Course of Action. One should decide what to do only after considering moral and pragmatic factors (Rest, 1986). Rest identified pragmatic factors as those that mean "sacrificing some personal interest or enduring some hardship" (p. 95).

The moral considerations that influence fraternity and sorority members include peer pressure, recruitment practices that emphasize quantity of new members, alcohol abuse, and dishonest academic practices such as cheating. Peer pressure often perpetuates unethical behaviors (Dalton and Petrie, 1997). Baier and Whipple (1990) found Greeks to be significantly more likely to conform to peers than non-Greeks. Students in leadership positions may have a clear sense of what should be done but may struggle with doing the right thing, because of how they think their peers will react. Fear of peers' rejection, retaliation, and alienation supersedes an interest in choosing ethical actions.

Pressure to recruit large numbers of members takes the focus away from recruiting members who embrace fraternal principles and who could help create and support a learning community. Some alumni and headquarters staff emphasize achieving a "quota," or a predetermined maximum number of new members. If students are not recruited on the basis of their commitment to the organization's educational and ethical ideals, it will be difficult for the leaders of Greek letter organizations to instill ethical decision-making processes in them.

Another moral aspect of Greek life is alcohol abuse. Astin (1996) revealed that those students likely to join fraternities consume more alcohol than those not interested in joining fraternities. If fraternities and sororities recruit new members whose interest in joining is informed by a desire to consume alcohol, they hamper their organizations' ability to foster ethical development (Willimon and Naylor, 1995).

Cheating is also a problem for fraternities and sororities, demonstrating further difficulties in selecting ethical courses of action. In a multicampus study of cheating, McCabe and Bowers (1996) found that fraternity and sorority members were significantly more likely to cheat on examinations than non-Greeks. The study also found that Greeks perceived their Greek peers as exhibiting only weak levels of disapproval toward cheating.

What can motivate fraternity and sorority members to choose the right, or moral, option when selecting a course of action? One suggestion for administrators who seek to influence Greeks' ethical decision making is to incorporate discussions of character and ethics in leadership education (Dalton and Petrie, 1997). The students in fraternity and sorority leadership roles need training to prepare them to do the right thing, despite the competing pressures. Current leadership offerings focus more on information dissemination and chapter operations. Such programs neglect the essential values-clarification component of leadership development. This kind of dialogue among fraternity and sorority student leaders places moral considerations at the center of the conversation. Furthermore, on many campuses, Greek communities are characterized as competitive, antagonistic, or indifferent toward each other. By talking about issues that matter, students from different Greek organizations develop relationships with each other. This creates an awareness of another community to which they all belong—the community of Greek life on their campus. According to Kohlberg (1984), the experience of living in "just and caring communities" can lead to moral commitment (quoted in Rest, 1986).

Students also must perceive a supportive environment for making ethical choices. Elements of this environment include clear institutional values that are expressed and lived consistently. "Institutions that clearly communicate core values and integrate those values into leadership practices and campus life are more likely to influence students' moral development. . . . What educators *do* must be consistent with what they *say*" (Dalton and Petrie, 1997, p. 23).

Implementing a Course of Action. The final component of moral behavior is "developing and implementing a plan of action (by) . . . working around impediments and unexpected difficulties, overcoming fatigue and frustrations, resisting detractions and other allurements, and keeping sight of the eventual goal" (Rest, 1986, p. 96). Acting out moral behavior requires inner strength (Rest, 1986); in short, "doing the right thing" demands courage and confidence in one's beliefs. As Roy Disney, one of the driving forces behind the Disney empire, once said, "It is not hard to make decisions when you know what your values are" (National Interfraternity Conference, 1995, p. 5).

Greek letter organizations can foster ethical actions by connecting their choices to the organization's cornerstone principles. Students must understand how to behave in ways consistent with principles of truth, justice, honor, respect, integrity, and community. Opportunities to talk about choices—such as whether to be honest or to lie, to challenge a wrong or to perpetuate it, to confront a member with a damaging personal problem or to deny that there is a problem—can provoke students to evaluate past choices. Other helpful opportunities include public debates about ethical matters, recognition and rewards for students who demonstrate commitment to the institution's ethical principles, occasions in which students take responsible roles in important campus issues, and community service activities (Dalton and Petrie, 1997).

To encourage the implementation of ethical decisions, one needs confrontation—redirecting behavior to bring about a desired positive change (National Interfraternity Conference Commission on Values and Ethics, 1992). When one knows the right thing and does not do it, friends—and institutions—have a duty to respond. A lack of response sends a message that it is acceptable to make an unethical choice, to deviate from stated Greek principles, to act in ways contrary to the learning community's values. For many Greeks, a distorted interpretation of friendship perpetuates the notion that one cannot confront another member because that person is a brother or sister. Thus, students should be taught that friendship requires confrontation; without confrontation, ethical lapses become accepted patterns of behavior.

Institutional leaders, including student affairs administrators, also have a responsibility to confront ethical and moral "lapses." Indeed, "Educators should tackle the negative effects of peer culture (alcohol and drug use, sexual exploitation, incivility, conformity, and materialism) head on through health education, human relations training, student conduct regulations, and peer interventions" (Dalton and Petrie, 1997).

Gender Differences in Ethical Development

The single-sex nature of fraternities and sororities has implications for the ethical development within these organizations. If gender differences exist in ethical development, senior student affairs officers and student affairs staff must be sensitive to such dynamics so as to understand how fraternity and sorority members may interpret their moral duties.

Kohlberg's research (1984) on moral reasoning, which was based on male subjects, revealed a moral orientation toward justice and fairness. An ethic of justice is concerned with being objective, being rational, and treating all parties fairly by fulfilling rules (Liddell, Halpin, and Halpin, 1993). Gilligan (1982) explored possible differences in women's moral development. The theme of her work articulates another orientation to morality—an ethic of caring for others. An ethic of care is characterized by intuition and responsiveness to others in a way that ensures that the least harm will be done and that no one will be left alone (Liddell, Halpin, and Halpin, 1993). Applying these two theories may mean approaching fraternities and sororities differently when addressing the problems associated with these organizations.

Other research (Ford and Lowery, 1986; Liddell, Halpin, and Halpin, 1993; Rest, 1986) has revealed no specific gender assignment to the ethics of care and justice. Instead, those studies found that individuals use both moral "voices" to a certain extent. It is critical to help students recognize that doing the least harm is as relevant as doing the right thing (Liddell, Halpin, and Halpin, 1993).

Student affairs administrators can help students reconcile these two moral dimensions and cultivate an ethic committed to principles *and* to people (Liddell, Halpin, and Halpin, 1993). Student affairs administrators can achieve this informally by helping students confront issues within their organizations. These administrators can accomplish this more formally through a self-governing judicial board. The organization's "moral voice," which is located in the founding principles, can ultimately guide both approaches.

Implications for Student Affairs Officers

If colleges and universities expect to foster a positive Greek experience on their campus, the senior student affairs officer must support the chapters in their efforts. To achieve their purposes, student organizations (including fraternities and sororities) need assistance, intervention, and role modeling from adults (including administrators, faculty, alumni, community officials, and parents). This group effort requires patience, individual and group accountability to the institution's educational mission, and active and firsthand involvement with Greek members.

To replace in loco parentis, Willimon and Naylor (1995) suggested a new framework for defining the relationships between students and institutions: *in loco amicis,* with the institution acting as "a wise friend" to the student. Such a friendship facilitates honest discourse and the debate of values and issues through "quality interaction concerning things that matter. . . . [Friendship] is the tough, long-term, often painful struggle to form community" (Willimon and Naylor, 1995, pp. 94–95). When values are debated, tested, demonstrated, and inculcated in a context of friendship, healthy confrontation, and (when necessary) stringent enforcement of rules, fraternities and sororities are held accountable to their ethical standards and to the educational priorities of the larger learning community.

References

Astin, A. *The American Freshman: National Norms for Fall, 1996.* Compiled by the staff of the Cooperative Educational Research Program, Higher Education Research Institute, Graduate School of Education, UCLA. Los Angeles: University of California, 1996.

Baier, J. L., and Whipple, E. G. "Greek Values and Attitudes: A Comparison with Independents." *NASPA Journal,* 1990, 28 (1), 43–53.

Center for the Advancement of Public Health. *Our Chapter, Our Choice: Final Evaluation Report.* Fairfax, Va.: George Mason University, 1996.

Cherrey, C. "Understanding and Shaping Organizational Culture." *Campus Activities Programming,* Apr. 1990, pp. 60–64.

Chickering, A. W. *Education and Identity.* San Francisco: Jossey-Bass, 1969.

Cousins, M. "Service Learning: A Tool for Citizenship and Career Development." *Vision and Action: The Newsletter of ACPA Commission I,* Summer 1994.

Dalton, J. C., and Petrie, A. M. "The Power of Peer Culture." *Educational Record,* 1997, 78 (3–4), 18–24.

Ford, M. R., and Lowery, C. R. "Gender Differences in Moral Reasoning: A Comparison of the Use of Justice and Care Orientations." *Journal of Personality and Social Psychology,* 1986, 50, 777–783.

Fraternity Insurance Purchasing Group. "Risk Management Policy." In *Interfraternity Directory.* Indianapolis, Ind.: National Interfraternity Conference, 1996.

Gilligan, C. *In a Different Voice: Psychological Theory and Women's Development.* Cambridge, Mass.: Harvard University Press, 1982.

Josephson, M. "Ethical Values, Attitudes, and Behaviors in American Schools." *Ethics: Easier Said Than Done, the Magazine of the Josephson Institute of Ethics,* 1992, 19, 35–45.

Kohlberg, L. *The Psychology of Moral Development.* San Francisco: Harper San Francisco, 1984.

Kohlberg, L., and Kramer, R. "Continuities and Discontinuities in Childhood and Adult Moral Development." *Human Development,* 1969, 12, 93–120.

Kuh, G. D., and Whitt, E. J. *The Invisible Tapestry: Culture in American Colleges and Universities.* Washington, D.C.: Asite Press, 1988.

Liddell, D. L., Halpin, G., and Halpin, W. G. "Men, Women, and Moral Orientation: Accounting for Our Differences." *NASPA Journal,* 1993, 30 (2), 138–144.

Linkenbach, J. *Our Chapter, Our Choice: Redefining Alcohol and Drug Norms Through Greek Empowerment.* Indianapolis, Ind.: National Interfraternity Conference, 1992.

Maisel, J. P. "Social Fraternities and Sororities Are Not Conducive to the Educational Process." *NASPA Journal,* 1990, 28 (1), 8–12.

McCabe, D. L., and Bowers, W. J. "The Relation Between Student Cheating and College Fraternity or Sorority Membership." *NASPA Journal,* 1996, 33 (4), 280–291.

National Interfraternity Conference. *Curriculum Brochure.* Indianapolis, Ind.: National Interfraternity Conference, 1995.

National Interfraternity Conference Commission on Values and Ethics (ed.). *Confrontation 101.* Indianapolis, Ind.: National Interfraternity Conference, 1992.

Pascarella, E. T., and Terenzini, P. T. *How College Affects Students: Findings and Insights from Twenty Years of Research.* San Francisco: Jossey-Bass, 1991.

Perry, W. "Cognitive and Ethical Growth: The Making of Meaning." In A. Chickering and Associates, *The Modern American College: Responding to the New Realities of Diverse Students and a Changing Society.* San Francisco: Jossey-Bass, 1981.

Rest, J. R. "Moral Development in Young Adults." In R. A. Mines and K. S. Kitchener (eds.), *Adult Cognitive Development.* New York: Praeger, 1986.

Rhoads, R. A. "Whales Tales, Dog Piles, and Beer Goggles: An Ethnographic Case Study of Fraternity Life." *Anthropology and Education Quarterly,* 1995, *26* (3), 306–323.

Shaw, D. L., and Morgan, T. E. "Greek Advisor's Perceptions of Sorority Hazing." *NASPA Journal,* 1990, *28* (1), 60–64.

Stombler, M., and Martin, P. Y. "Bringing Women In, Keeping Women Down: Fraternity 'Little Sister' Organizations." *Journal of Contemporary Ethnography,* 1994, *23* (2), 150–184.

Wechsler, H., Kuh, G. D., and Davenport, A. E. "Fraternities, Sororities, and Binge Drinking: Results from a National Study of American Colleges." *NASPA Journal,* 1996, *33* (4), 260–279.

Wilbur, J. "Greek Affiliation in College Contributes Positively to Community Involvement." *Campus Commentary,* March 1997, Issue 7, p. 1.

Willimon, W. H., and Naylor, T. H. *The Abandoned Generation: Rethinking Higher Education.* Grand Rapids, Mich.: Eerdmans, 1995.

CATHY EARLEY is director of leadership education for the National Interfraternity Conference. Prior to her employment there, she served as coordinator of Greek affairs at Washington University in St. Louis.

To address the persistent challenge of Greek alcohol abuse, campus administrators must work with Greek letter organizations to establish effective alcohol policies and programs that promote alcohol awareness and responsible use.

Greek Letter Organizations and Alcohol: Problems, Policies, and Programs

Bridget Guernsey Riordan, Robert Q. Dana

College presidents have ranked alcohol abuse as the primary problem on campus for years (Boyer, 1990; Eigen, 1991; Wechsler, 1996). In 1998, the problems associated with alcohol abuse still dwarf other social considerations on U.S. campuses. Alcohol is the most widely used drug among college students. Studies show almost unbelievable rates of alcoholic consumption on college campuses. Students in Greek letter organizations are at particular risk for alcohol abuse. "The biggest predictor of binge drinking in college is residency in a fraternity or sorority. That's number one by far" (Philpott, 1997b, p. 6). This chapter will describe some of the research on alcohol use on campuses, especially by Greeks, and then suggest ways in which student affairs officers and Greek organizations can address this challenge.

The Nature of the Challenge

During an academic year, 85 percent of students consume alcohol. Of these students, 50 percent are binge drinkers (Wechsler, 1996). They drink frequently, and when they drink, they become drunk. Alcohol is a significant factor in physical violence, unwanted and regretted sex, sexual assault, automobile accidents, academic failure, social failure, and damage to residence halls and Greek living units (Anchors and Dana, 1992; Kuh and Arnold, 1992; Dana, Pratt, Kochis, and Andrews, 1993; Wechsler, 1996). Clearly, alcohol abuse is a corrosive influence in a learning community.

Students are quick to state that they choose to become intoxicated because they like the feeling, they want to have fun with their friends, or they are bored. According to Grayson and Cauley (1989, p. 194), "Students drink

NEW DIRECTIONS FOR STUDENT SERVICES, no. 81, Spring 1998 © Jossey-Bass Publishers

because alcohol serves many developmental functions in the college setting." These functions include experimenting with different identities without lasting commitment, creating a sense of belonging, experimenting with sexual relationships, and coping with stress and feelings of inadequacy (Grayson and Cauley, 1989). These are, of course, only short-term and ultimately ineffective strategies for dealing with developmental issues, but it is necessary to recognize that alcohol plays an important role in helping students manage the uncertainties of their life stage.

Students are likely to deny that their alcohol use is problematic, and they often refuse to accept that negative consequences could occur. Henry Weschler, a researcher who studies college student drinking, has noted that "denial is a very important feature of problem drinking. . . . [Students who abuse alcohol] don't think it's a problem so they don't listen" (Philpott, 1997b, p. 5).

Fraternity and sorority membership increases the likelihood that a student will abuse alcohol. In fact, "virtually every study of drinking in college shows that fraternity members tend to drink more heavily and more frequently and to have more alcohol-related problems than their fellow students" (Wechsler, Kuh, and Davenport, 1996, p. 261). Much of this drinking occurs in environments that are difficult to control and during situations in which heavy drinking is normative. A 1996 multicampus study of student alcohol use found that 80 percent of sorority residents and 86 percent of fraternity residents were binge drinkers. That is, at least once in a two-week period, the men consumed five or more drinks in a row and the women consumed four or more drinks in a row (Wechsler, 1996). Of Greeks who did not reside in a chapter house, 71 percent of fraternity members and 58 percent of sorority members were binge drinkers. Another recent study found that leaders of fraternities and, to a lesser degree, sororities were among the worst offenders. These student leaders were most likely to report having had a hangover, arguing or fighting, getting in trouble with police or campus authorities, driving while under the influence, getting sick, or missing a class (Marklein, 1997). Sadly, these are the students who should be most concerned about problems related to alcohol abuse and the serious consequences this abuse has for Greek letter organizations, members, and institutions. In contrast, only 45 percent of non-Greek men and 35 percent of non-Greek women were binge drinkers (Wechsler, Kuh, and Davenport, 1996).

An additional problem is fraternity or sorority hazing involving the use of alcohol. Ninety percent of hazing deaths are related to alcohol abuse (Eigen, 1991). During the first six weeks of the school year in 1997, as we wrote this chapter, two fraternity deaths involving alcohol and hazing were reported in the national media.

Researchers have offered several explanations for the strong and significant relationship between Greek membership and problem drinking. In a 1997 interview, Henry Wechsler of the Harvard School of Public Health College Alcohol Study noted that Greek letter organizations not only attract students who are already abusing alcohol but also seem to cause alcohol abuse. Wechsler stated that fraternities and sororities "attract more binge drinkers proportionately to the general population of college students, and they help create drinkers, particularly women. However, the men were already binge drinking at higher levels than nonfraternity men while they were in high school, while the women were at about the same levels before [college] as nonsorority women" (Philpott, 1997b, pp. 6–7).

Others have speculated that the process of inducting new members is an important factor in alcohol abuse among Greeks. Many colleges and universities permit students to join fraternities and sororities at the beginning of the first year in college, a time when new students are particularly susceptible to peer pressure. Thus, "when used in combination with hazing episodes, alcohol becomes interwoven into a complicated system of rewards and sanctions to which newcomers must conform . . . and learn to become loyal to the group in resisting external threats, including institutional sanctions" (Wechsler, Kuh, and Davenport, 1996, p. 275). Therefore, a second explanation for the rate of problem drinking in fraternities and sororities is that "powerful conformist cultures" socialize new members through the use of alcohol (Wechsler, Kuh, and Davenport, 1996, p. 275).

The consequences of alcohol abuse for individual students, Greek organizations, and institutions are severe, ranging from missed classes to property damage to death (Wechsler, 1996). Ultimately, alcohol abuse contradicts the values of higher education and inhibits the development of communities of learners. Indeed, it inhibits student learning (Pascarella and others, 1996).

Colleges and universities are aware of these problems and of their responsibility to help students learn to make good decisions about alcohol use. Many institutions have, for example, implemented substance abuse prevention programs designed to decrease the negative effects of drinking, increase student awareness of the problems associated with alcohol use, and provide alternatives to alcohol abuse.

To be effective, alcohol abuse prevention programs should focus on providing more adaptive and successful long-term solutions to the developmental complexities that college students face. In the remainder of this chapter, we offer suggestions for colleges and universities seeking to address this challenge.

Institutional Approaches to Alcohol Problems

Because the culture of alcohol use and abuse in Greek organizations is so pervasive and debilitating, "decisive institutional action is needed by presidents, student affairs administrators, and group advisors" (Wechsler, Kuh, and Davenport, 1996, p. 275). No single approach will be effective, however, and any programs or policies suggested here must be adapted to the needs of individual campuses.

One multifaceted model for an institutional response to alcohol abuse in Greek letter organizations is Wechsler's *Twelve-Step Program* (Wechsler, 1996;

Philpott, 1997a). This program provides a framework for campuses to use in defining their particular alcohol-related problems and in articulating institutional values and expectations for community members. The *Twelve-Step Program* includes the following:

- An assessment of alcohol's impact on campus
- Public acknowledgment that there is an alcohol problem at the institution
- The college president's leadership in alcohol prevention and intervention efforts
- Commitment to a long-term change process
- Everyone's involvement (including faculty, students, administrators, athletic staff, local community members, and alumni) in the change effort
- A clear and consistently enforced code of student conduct that states regulations about alcohol use, the consequences of problem drinking, and the rights of students who do not abuse alcohol
- Confrontation of others' alcohol abuse by members of fraternities and sororities
- Academic policies (for example, Friday classes and examinations) that discourage alcohol abuse
- Clear expectations communicated from a student's first contact with the college (for example, "We do not offer a major in binge drinking" (Philpott, 1997a, p. 15)
- Plentiful assistance for problem drinkers

Creating Institutional Policies on Alcohol Use. Many institutions have modeled their alcohol policies after the *Model Alcohol Policy* created in 1985 by the Inter-Association Task Force on Campus Alcohol Issues (Boost Alcohol Consciousness Concerning the Health of University Students, 1986). This group, which was later renamed the Inter-Association Task Force on Alcohol and Other Substance Abuse Issues, brought together representatives of many higher education associations, including the National Association of Student Personnel Administrators, the American College Personnel Association, the National Interfraternity Conference (NIC), and the United States Student Association.

The *Model Alcohol Policy* identified elements essential to any effective campus alcohol policy (Boost Alcohol Consciousness Concerning the Health of University Students, 1986). These are as follows:

- A statement of institutional educational values and expectations for community members' actions
- A summary of relevant local and state laws
- Clear regulations regarding alcohol use (including where alcoholic beverages may be possessed, served, consumed, and sold); guidelines for private and public social events (for example, advertising, security, and the sale or distribution of alcohol); rules about alcohol use at recruitment activities and ath-

letic events; and guidelines for marketing and advertising campus events involving alcohol
- Judicial procedures and sanctions for violations of alcohol policies

Just as the components of an institution's alcohol policy are important, the process of creating the policy is equally important. To formulate and implement an effective alcohol policy requires extensive student input and involvement (Astin, 1984; Gehring, 1986; Nelson, 1987). If students feel that they own the policy because they have participated in its development, that will help to disseminate and enforce the policy.

Alumni can also help Greek organizations address the problems that their chapter members face with alcohol. Student affairs professionals must solicit alumni to help members understand the impact of alcohol abuse, particularly as it pertains to academic achievement and career opportunities (Wechsler, Kuh, and Davenport, 1996). They can do this by sharing data about the amount and frequency of alcohol use by Greeks and by providing examples of the negative consequences of such behavior.

Not all alumni will address problem drinking productively, however. Those who do not choose to help curb alcohol misuse should be removed from advising the chapters. Alumni members who do realize the need for strong alcohol education can have a positive influence and can help the members change their culture (Wechsler, Kuh, and Davenport, 1996).

If the alumni and university officials are unable to change the chapter culture by educating the members and changing the house environment, the only alternative may be to remove from the organization those members who cannot live up to its standards. If the misuse of alcohol is unalterably etched into a chapter's culture, the only recourse may be to remove the organization from the institution altogether (Wechsler, Kuh, and Davenport, 1996). Alumni involvement and support of this decision can be useful and should be sought, as alumni can help implement the necessary measures.

Some institutions have decided that the best way to prevent alcohol problems is to prohibit its use on campus. This may be unrealistic, however, and may create other problems, such as moving drinking to off-campus locations (Nelson, 1979). Institutions that prohibit alcohol entirely miss the opportunity to help students learn to make responsible choices. Furthermore, there is historical evidence that complete prohibition of alcohol in society cannot be enforced (Roberts and Novak, 1986). Basic risk management strategies indicate that policies should not be on the books unless the institution can clearly and efficiently enforce them. At the same time, schools without a policy on alcohol may breach their "duty to care," thereby leaving themselves vulnerable to lawsuits (Gulland and Flournoy, 1985, p. 20).

Campus administrators, then, must strike a balance between "the educational ideals of the student affairs professional and the counsel of the university attorney" (Letzring and Holcomb, 1996, p. 79). By doing so, they can create policies that support the institution's educational purposes and values while minimizing legal risks. Additional information about the legal implications of alcohol policies appears in Chapter Six.

Coordinating Institutional Policies with Greek Headquarters. Greek letter organizations are governed by Interfraternity and Panhellenic Council policies, which often have specific guidelines for parties with alcohol. In addition, the headquarters of each Greek letter organization has its own policy on alcohol use. Up-to-date copies of each chapter's policies should be on file with the appropriate administrative office.

Many headquarters comply with the risk management policies established by the Fraternity Insurance Purchasing Group (FIPG), a consortium of national and international Greek organizations formed to minimize legal liabilities and obtain insurance for their chapters. These FIPG policies use basic risk management practices that allow organizations to serve alcohol at parties but to do so in a legal and responsible manner (Fraternity Insurance Purchasing Group, 1996). Because these policies were established by the groups themselves and apply to all of their collegiate chapters, the officers and advisers of those groups are responsible for enforcing them. An FIPG board investigates reports of any risk management violations that involve their member organizations. Senior student affairs officers and Greek advisers can therefore turn to the FIPG board as an ally in assisting with risk management compliance.

Because fraternities and sororities are subject to the policies and regulations of their institutions, their Interfraternity and Panhellenic Councils, and their national or international organization, they may be governed by three or more alcohol policies. Therefore, it is important that the policies complement one another so that chapters do not receive mixed messages. An institution can ensure this by including provisions from the fraternity or sorority policies in its own policies. For instance, if a national policy mandates that no alcohol be present at new member events, then the institution should state that in its policy. Legally, each group (the institution, headquarters, and governing organization) can only be responsible for enforcing its own policy. Thus, they should include similar provisions and values to enforce, even though it may appear redundant. If one policy governing a group is stricter than another, the group must always follow the more stringent policy components in order to comply with every policy.

Strategies for Primary Prevention and Alcohol Education

Although comprehensive policies and consistent enforcement are intended to prevent misuse of alcohol, recent research shows that institutional alcohol policies alone do not have a discernible effect on the drinking patterns and problems reported by students (Hanson and Engs, 1995). Because of this, additional approaches to reducing alcohol abuse are needed, including prevention and education programs and efforts designed to change student cultures (Gonzalez, 1991). More resources must be allocated for these efforts than has traditionally been the case (Gonzalez, 1991). This may include funding for alternative campus programming that does not include alcoholic beverages, as well as for educational programs and primary prevention efforts.

Primary Prevention. *Primary prevention* refers to activities that reduce or stabilize the incidence (new cases) of substance abuse or related problems and thereby reduce or stabilize its prevalence (the total number of cases). In other words, primary prevention programs are designed to stop a problem from developing. Because of the complexities of alcohol use and abuse, it is not easy to create and implement college-based substance abuse prevention programs (Lewis, Dana, and Blevins, 1994). To be effective, such prevention strategies should be comprehensive, extensive, and relevant (Berkowitz, 1990; Enos and Pittayathikhun, 1997).

Comprehensive prevention strategies involve students, staff, and faculty; give students exposure to prevention in multiple settings from a variety of sources; and eliminate inconsistent messages. Extensive efforts provide exposure to anti-abuse messages over a period of time rather than in a one-shot experience, and they require active participation rather than passive attendance. Messages will seem more relevant if they are tailored to specific groups and if they focus on immediate negative consequences (such as injury, sexually transmitted diseases, and acquaintance rape) rather than drinking's long-term health risks. In general, effective prevention strategies use peer education to take advantage of the power of peer influence, integrate survey research, teach students to help themselves (for example, through assertiveness training and goal setting), and work on changing the immediate social environment (Berkowitz, 1990; Enos and Pittayathikhun, 1997).

Another effective concept that many institutions use to address alcohol behavior is the prevention contract (Hunnicutt, Davis, and Fletcher, 1991). The prevention contract allows students to document an intolerable behavior, such as driving while drunk or missing a class because of alcohol. Students can then take a stand against this behavior. The contract is not meant to be legally binding but rather to reinforce a personal commitment from each student who signs it. Prevention contracts can create a basis from which university administrators, Greek leaders, and chapter members can work cooperatively to address concerns and problems associated with alcohol misuse (Hunnicutt, Davis, and Fletcher, 1991). Because the law often places institutions and students in a contractual relationship as a replacement to the in loco parentis doctrine, the prevention contract is a suitable method in this often complicated and ever changing student and university relationship (Letzring and Holcomb, 1996).

Headquarters staff, along with institutional personnel, can develop prevention education programs that encourage Greek members to find alternatives to alcohol while alerting them to the risks of excessive alcohol consumption (Tampke, 1990). Together, Greek headquarters and institutions can define a sense of community that helps students recognize their obligation to conduct themselves in responsible ways (Pavela, 1992). By combining resources with the headquarters, institutions can also open the channels of communication and share the costs of program development and implementation.

Alcohol Education. In an examination of cutting-edge approaches to alcohol education, Walton (1996) identified possible strategies for student affairs professionals. These address a wide range of alcohol issues while supporting the development of a caring, learning community. According to Walton, the ideal comprehensive alcohol education program includes a written alcohol policy, informational seminars about drunk driving and local liquor statutes, seminars about social host liability, workshops to train party servers, a health-oriented class about alcoholism and mature drinking, an annual "alcohol awareness" month, a college-sponsored safe transportation program, a written statement discussing possible judicial procedures for alcohol violations, and an alcohol counseling program.

Some fraternity and sorority headquarters staff or alumni volunteers educate their members through programs that measure the extent to which an individual has a drinking problem. One widely used program is *On Campus Talking About Alcohol,* developed by the Prevention Research Initiative Institute in Lexington, Kentucky. This eight-hour, research-based risk reduction course is designed to help participants assess their own level of risk for alcoholism. They base this assessment on the quantity and frequency of consumption and the family history of alcoholism. After participating in the program, participants receive guidelines on how to change high-risk behaviors and to begin consuming alcohol in a low-risk way.

Peer Alcohol Education. An organization named Boost Alcohol Consciousness Concerning the Health of University Students (BACCHUS) and another one named Greeks Advocating the Mature Management of Alcohol (GAMMA) Peer Education Network were established in 1975. These are the main sources of alcohol resource materials and alcohol educational programs for colleges and universities. Since its inception, BACCHUS has evolved from merely an alcohol awareness organization to a peer education network committed to educating, training, and supporting peer educators. More than 750 campuses have BACCHUS chapters that advocate informed, independent decision making and respect for state laws and campus policies. National Collegiate Alcohol Awareness Week is the most widely recognized activity of BACCHUS chapters.

GAMMA denotes BACCHUS chapters with a special emphasis on peer education for fraternities and sororities. Fraternity and sorority members throughout the nation use BACCHUS's resources—including videos, pamphlets, posters, manuals, and promotional materials—to educate members on diverse topics, including alcohol poisoning, addiction, and sex under the influence. Headquartered at the University of Denver, BACCHUS and GAMMA have a membership exceeding 24,000 collegians.

In addition to using BACCHUS and GAMMA, the NIC staff members use peer education efforts to change chapter cultures. Through the *Our Chapter,*

Our Choice program, NIC tries to modify student drinking behaviors. Trained facilitators come to campuses to educate students about using the theories set forth in the program to adjust student norms and help students make more responsible choices about alcohol consumption. The facilitators train the student leaders to be facilitators within Greek letter organizations. Chapters invite the facilitators in to do the program only after 80 percent of the chapter has voted to participate in it. Trained student leaders help fellow students examine their current norms of drinking behaviors and assist them in reshaping those norms for healthier decision making and lifestyles. This allows the students to own the program and to do problem solving themselves.

Aside from the peer education programs established through BACCHUS and the NIC, many campuses have found success working with their own campus counseling departments or health education departments. They have developed peer education programs that effectively deal with alcohol education issues on their campuses. Institutions such as California State University-Long Beach, Arizona State University, the University of Maryland, the University of Denver, and the University of Southern California have developed effective alcohol awareness programs on their campuses.

At California State University-Long Beach, for example, Students for Health Awareness, Resources, and Knowledge (SHARK) was created through the collaboration of the Greek letter organizations and the Office of Student Life and Development. Through SHARK, students participate in group exercises that explore the scope of leadership responsibilities within the Greek system, as well as key issues that affect members and influence other people's perceptions of Greeks.

National Collegiate Alcohol Awareness Week at the University of Denver took on special significance when it fell during Homecoming Week. Members of the GAMMA chapter, as well as the Department of Residence Life and the group called Students Taking an Active Role Together, created activities such as Dead Out Day and a day of abstaining from alcohol. On Dead Out Day, students volunteered to be dead from a drunk driving accident and did not speak to anyone the entire day. This demonstrated how the loss of close friends would affect others. During the day of abstinence, more than 250 students took the pledge to abstain from alcohol consumption for a twenty-four-hour period.

Concluding Thoughts

Greek letter organizations must confront the problem of alcohol abuse among their members. Although statistics on the success of any student education program are dismal, the numbers are especially gloomy for fraternities and sororities. College students are at high risk for developing alcohol problems and for experiencing negative outcomes associated with the immoderate use of alcohol. According to Eigen (1991), college students appear to be at particularly high risk compared with other drinking groups, and fraternity and sorority members are at still higher risk.

The picture is disturbing but not hopeless. There are opportunities for reform and change at campuses across this country. Student affairs professionals play an important role in alcohol abuse prevention among student populations (Enos and Pittayathikhun, 1997), and success is more likely if campuses work as communities to solve this community problem. It may seem easier to pass off the problems of Greeks and alcohol abuse to a Greek adviser or a campus substance abuse program, but this is a simple solution to a complex problem. Collaboration across a campus and throughout student and community groups will lead to the development of a comprehensive, multi-level approach that will stand the test of time (Enos and Pittayathikhun, 1997).

There are no simple solutions. The problems of alcohol abuse are complex, and a successful response to these issues should be developmentally sensitive and dynamic. As students and campuses change, so too should approaches to the challenge of student alcohol abuse.

References

Anchors, W. S., and Dana, R. Q. "Substance Abuse Patterns and Personality Type Among First Year Residence Hall Students: A Two Year Study." *Journal of College and University Housing,* 1992, 22 (1), 26–31.

Astin, A. W. "Student Involvement: A Developmental Theory for Higher Education." *Journal of College Student Personnel,* 1984, 25 (4), 297–308.

Berkowitz, A. "Reducing Alcohol and Other Drug Abuse on Campus: Effective Strategies for Prevention Programs." *Eta Sigma Gamma,* 1990, 22 (1), 12–14.

Boost Alcohol Consciousness Concerning the Health of University Students (BACCHUS). Proceedings of BACCHUS of the United States's First National Conference on Campus Alcohol Policy Initiatives, Gainesville, Fla., July 1986.

Boyer, E. *Campus Life: In Search of Community.* Princeton, N.J.: Princeton University Press and Carnegie Foundation for the Advancement of Teaching, 1990.

Dana, R. Q., Pratt, P., Kochis, R., and Andrews, W. "Problematic College Drinking Behaviors as a Function of First Intoxication." *Journal of Alcohol and Drug Education,* 1993, 38 (2), 92–99.

Eigen, L. "Alcohol Practices, Policies, and Potentials of American Colleges and Universities: A White Paper." Washington, D.C.: Office of Substance Abuse Prevention, U.S. Department of Health and Human Services, 1991.

Enos, T., and Pittayathikhun, T. *Alcohol and Other Drug Prevention: A Bulletin for Fraternity and Sorority Advisers.* Washington, D.C.: Higher Education Center for Alcohol and Other Drug Prevention, U.S. Department of Education, 1997.

Fraternity Insurance Purchasing Group. "Risk Management Policy." In *Interfraternity Directory.* Indianapolis, Ind.: National Interfraternity Conference, 1996.

Gehring, D. D. "Dramshop and Social Host Liability and Its Impact on Higher Education." Paper presented at BACCHUS of the United States's First National Conference on Campus Alcohol Policy Initiatives, Gainesville, Fla., July 1986.

Gonzalez, G. M. "Effects of Awareness and Legal Drinking Age on Alcohol Knowledge, Consumption, and Problems." *NASPA Journal,* 1991, 28 (3), 243–250.

Grayson, P., and Cauley, K. *College Psychotherapy.* New York: Guilford, 1989.

Gulland, E. E., and Flournoy, A. C. *Universities, Colleges and Alcohol: An Overview of Tort Liability Issues.* White Paper on Student Alcohol Abuse. Washington, D.C.: American Council on Education, 1985.

Hanson, D. J., and Engs, R. C. "Collegiate Drinking: Administrator Perception, Campus Policies, and Student Behaviors." *NASPA Journal,* 1995, 32 (2), 106–114.

Hunnicutt, D. M., Davis, J. L., and Fletcher, J. "Preventing Alcohol Abuse in the Greek System on a Commuter Campus: Prevention Contracts." *NASPA Journal,* 1991, *28* (1), 179–184.

Kuh, G. D., and Arnold, J. C. *Brotherhood and the Bottle: A Cultural Analysis of the Role of Alcohol in Fraternities.* Bloomington: Center for the Study of the College Fraternity, Indiana University, 1992.

Letzring, T. D., and Holcomb, T. "Liability, Alcohol, and Student Conduct Codes: Balancing Student and Institutional Rights." *College Student Affairs Journal,* 1996, *15* (2), 74–86.

Lewis, J., Dana, R. Q., and Blevins, G. *Substance Abuse Counseling: An Individualized Approach.* (2nd ed.) Pacific Grove, Calif.: Brooks/Cole, 1994.

Marklein, M. "Fraternity, Sorority Leaders Are Among Heaviest Drinkers." *USA Today,* Dec. 16, 1997, p. 1A.

Nelson, S. J. "Alcohol Use on the College Campus: Some Ethical Implications." *NASPA Journal,* 1979, *16* (4), 2–6.

Nelson, S. J. "Alcohol Policies and Educational Mission." *NASPA Journal,* 1987, *25* (2), 91–97.

Pascarella, E. T., Edison, M., Whitt, E. J., Nora, A., Hagedorn, L. S., and Terenzini, P. T. "Cognitive Effects of Greek Affiliation During the First Year of College." *NASPA Journal,* 1996, *33* (4), 242–259.

Pavela, G. "Today's College Students Need Both Freedom and Structure." *Chronicle of Higher Education,* 1992, *38* (47), B1–B2.

Philpott, J. "Facing Up to Our Campus Drinking Problem: The View from Campus." *About Campus,* 1997a, *2* (2), 9–15.

Philpott, J. "Facing Up to Our Campus Drinking Problem: What We Know." (Interview with Henry Weschler.) *About Campus,* 1997b, *2* (2), 4–8.

Roberts, D. C., and Novak, A. J. "Implications of the Change to a Minimum Drinking Age of Twenty-One for the College Environment." *Journal of College Student Personnel,* 1986, *27* (6), 484–490.

Tampke, D. R. "Alcohol Behavior, Risk Perception, and Fraternity and Sorority Membership." *NASPA Journal,* 1990, *28* (1), 71–77.

Walton, S. "Social Host Liability: Risks for Fraternities and Student Hosts." *NASPA Journal,* 1996, *34* (1), 29–35.

Wechsler, H. "Alcohol and the American College Campus: A Report from the Harvard School of Public Health." *Change,* July–Aug. 1996, pp. 20–60.

Wechsler, H., Kuh, G. D., and Davenport, A. E. "Fraternities, Sororities, and Binge Drinking: Results from a National Study of American Colleges." *NASPA Journal,* 1996, *33* (4), 260–279.

BRIDGET GUERNSEY RIORDAN *is assistant to the vice president and dean for campus life at Emory University. Her initial work in student affairs was as the coordinator of Greek affairs at the University of Cincinnati.*

ROBERT Q. DANA *is associate dean of students and community life at the University of Maine. He is directly responsible for Health Promotion and Prevention Services, which includes programs in AIDS and HIV prevention, community health nursing, preventive medicine, peer programs, sexual assault awareness, and the University of Maine Substance Abuse Services.*

Institutions of higher education, as well as the Greek letter organizations they host, are under increasing public and legal scrutiny. It is vital that student affairs administrators understand and address the potential legal implications of having Greek organizations on their campuses.

Legal Issues and Greek Letter Organizations

Nicholas J. Hennessy, Lisa M. Huson

Experiences in out-of-class activities, both on and off campus, can contribute to learning and personal development (Astin, 1993; Pascarella and Terenzini, 1991; Terenzini, Pascarella, and Blimling, 1996). Greek letter organizations can motivate their members to undertake educationally purposeful activities and can foster effective environments for learning (Kuh, 1996). These organizations can also impede learning, though (Kuh, Pascarella, and Wechsler, 1996; Maisel, 1990).

The activities of some organizations and their members put both the groups and their institutions at legal risk. Colleges and universities are experiencing pressure to increase their accountability for achieving educational goals to various groups, including local, state, and federal legislators; students; parents; and the public. It is clear that such Greek system activities as hazing, using alcohol to excess, and sexually assaulting women, as well as the liability issues they generate, neither help create a learning community nor contribute to desired educational outcomes.

In lawsuits against Greek letter organizations, many of the potential defendants tend to be "judgment-proof." (That is, they do not own sufficient property to forfeit much of value if they lose the suit.) Therefore, institutions become likely targets for the litigation. Higher education administrators must be familiar with risk reduction and risk management.

Although the details and mechanics of risk management are often the purview of administrators other than student affairs professionals, senior student affairs officers' ability to make decisions informed by risk management and liability considerations will be of great use to their institutions. Institutions with Greek letter organizations have decided that those organizations contribute to the institution's mission. To continue to realize those contributions, all parties need to work together to eliminate the legal risks that these organizations pose.

The purpose of this chapter is to acquaint senior student affairs officers with some of the basic legal challenges that have been and could be encountered in connection with Greek letter organizations on their campuses. Of particular concern here is the way in which the law views the relationship between the institution and the student, as well as what the institution must do to fulfill its legal duty to provide for students' safety. From a legal perspective, the chapter will analyze specific negative practices of some Greek letter organizations and their members, including hazing, misusing alcohol, and sexually assaulting women. We hope the information presented in this chapter will help senior student affairs officers make informed decisions about Greek organizations and the institution's liability so that they can strike an appropriate balance between the enhancement of educational values and the elimination of liability issues.

Before proceeding, however, we must offer a caveat. At no time should the information in this chapter be considered legal advice. Rather, we present ideas and issues to be examined within an institutional context and with appropriate legal advice. A college or university is fundamentally different from other corporate entities, as it has an educational mission, roles, and constituents. Its legal issues therefore pose distinct challenges for senior student affairs officers and other administrators. These cannot be analyzed in a legal vacuum.

General Liability Issues

In general, higher education institutions do not stand in loco parentis to the students on their campuses. That is, they do not assume a duty to protect students from harm. This is the case whether the Greek organizations are housed on campus, are housed off campus, or are not housed at all by the institution.

There was a time when college administrators and faculties assumed such a role. A special relationship was thought to exist between the institution and student. This relationship imposed a duty on the institution to exercise control over students' conduct, and it gave students certain rights of protection by the institution (Kaplin and Lee, 1995). College campuses have changed, however. A reapportionment of responsibilities and social interests has lessened the duty of protection that institutions once owed students. For example, college administrators no longer control students' general morals (Kaplin and Lee, 1995). Thus, institutions' legal risk for students' actions is more favorable. Institutions have more leeway now than in the days of in loco parentis.

When the actions of Greek letter organizations have caused injuries to individuals, most attempts to hold institutions accountable have failed (Paine, 1994). Courts have recognized that colleges and universities neither function as insurers of student safety nor generally stand in a special relationship with students. The relationship between the student and the institution is defined by applicable state law and is subject to interpretation by the courts. Thus, this relationship differs across states and across court jurisdictions.

Nevertheless, a liability claim or the mere threat of litigation against the institution can often be as devastating from the standpoint of monetary and human resources as an actual lawsuit. Attorneys' fees for dealing with claims, time lost through staff involvement in administrative and legal procedures, and high settlement figures are just some of the debilitating aspects of threatened litigation. No senior student affairs officer or any other administrator desires such negative effects, whether the lawsuit is won, lost, or settled out of court.

The majority of legal claims against Greek letter organizations are for torts, or civil wrongs, other than breach of contract, for which the courts will allow a damage remedy. Torts include negligence—injury to another caused by failure to maintain a standard of care for that person. An example of a tort claim is a suit by a person who was hurt when he fell from the roof of a fraternity house after becoming intoxicated at a party hosted there. This scenario has legal implications for the fraternity. Depending on whether or not the university houses the chapter, it might also have similar implications for the institution.

According to basic tort law, an institution can only be liable for negligence if it has a duty to minimize any conduct that could threaten students' physical or mental safety. If the institution does not have the obligation to protect students from dangerous behavior by Greek letter organizations, then the victim has no recourse against the institution, even if it can be said that the institution acted negligently (Bickel, 1996). Other elements required for a legal finding of negligence include a failure to fulfill the duty, a causal connection between the Greek letter organization or its members' conduct and the injury, and an actual loss or damage that was sustained as a result of the injury (Kaplin and Lee, 1995).

Because institutions are legally separate from Greek letter organizations, the institution generally owes them, their members, and others only an ordinary duty of care to avoid injuring others—that is, a duty to act "reasonably" to prevent harm. This is the same level of duty owed a trespasser of land, not a standard of care associated with a special relationship between the institution and its students. A "special relationship" might be found within the context of a landlord/tenant relationship, in connection with the sponsorship of intercollegiate sports, or based on certain written contracts (Kaplin and Lee, 1995).

Since the landmark case of *Bradshaw* v. *Rawlings,* 612 F.2d 135 (Pa. 1979), courts in many jurisdictions have recognized that colleges and universities neither function as insurers of student safety nor generally stand in a special relationship with students. In that case, a student, Bradshaw, was seriously injured in an automobile accident after the annual sophomore class picnic, which was held off campus. The injured student was riding in a car driven by an underage student who had become intoxicated at the picnic by drinking beer purchased with class funds. The plaintiffs alleged that a special relationship between the institution and Bradshaw had been created by the college's written regulation prohibiting the possession or consumption of alcoholic beverages on campus or off campus at college-sponsored functions. The regulation followed the state law prohibiting persons under the age of twenty-one from drinking alcohol. Thus, the *Bradshaw* court found that the institution had only reaffirmed the necessity of student compliance with state law. It had not voluntarily taken "custody" of Bradshaw so as to be under a duty to protect him from the consumption of alcohol (Kaplin and Lee, 1995).

Ever since *Bradshaw,* colleges and universities have maintained that students' adult status deprives colleges of the authority to regulate and control student behavior. *Rabel* v. *Illinois Wesleyan University,* 514 N.E.2d 522 (Ill. App. Ct. 1987) illustrated this principle. Rabel, a student, was grabbed in her residence hall by an intoxicated member of a male Greek letter organization. After being dragged outside by the male student, she suffered a serious head injury when she fell onto the sidewalk. Rabel sued the Greek letter organization and the institution, alleging that the institution was aware of excessive drinking in this organization at the time of the incident and in the past. She sought damages for the institution's negligence in failing to make reasonable efforts to enforce its prohibition of alcohol on campus (Bickel, 1996). The court, however, found that the mere foreseeability of injury to the plaintiff was not a sufficient reason to obligate the institution to reduce the risk of harm to students. Citing *Bradshaw,* the court concluded that college rules that prohibit alcohol consumption by underage students do not create a custodial relationship between the college and its students. Therefore, the college had no duty to minimize the risk of injuries such as those suffered by Rabel (Bickel, 1996).

On the other hand, some courts have departed from *Bradshaw* and viewed institutional attempts to regulate the conduct of Greek organization members (for example, alcohol consumption or other activities) as an assumption of a duty to control their behavior (Kaplin and Lee, 1995). In *Furek* v. *University of Delaware,* 594 A.2d 506 (Del. 1991), a new fraternity member suffered burns when oven cleaner was poured on him during hazing. This injury took place in the chapter house, which was leased from the university. In an opinion contrary to *Bradshaw,* the court questioned the idea that students are responsible for their own safety simply because they are adults and the notion that this adult status makes the institution's intrusion into alcohol-related activities inappropriate (Bickel, 1996). Indeed, the court found a duty on the part of the institution to protect students against the hazards inherent in hazing, and it decided that the institution breached this duty. The University of Delaware had adopted a specific policy against hazing. This convinced the court that if the institution failed to exercise reasonable care to enforce the policy, and if this failure resulted in injuries, the institution was liable. The institution knew of hazing's danger, stated openly that it would not permit such acts, and then did nothing to intervene when it had the opportunity to prevent injury. It therefore became liable for Furek's injuries (Bickel, 1996).

Inasmuch as *Furek* was a federal district court case, it is binding law only within that judicial district. It is only persuasive authority in other jurisdictions. Although *Furek* may not be the law in every judicial district, it points out the potential dangers of institutional attempts to regulate the conduct of Greek letter organizations and their members. Such attempts might be viewed as an assumption of a duty to control their behavior with a corresponding obligation to do so (Bickel, 1996). Kaplin and Lee (1995) suggested that certain institutional actions (such as inspecting kitchens and chapter houses, requiring that there be faculty and staff advisers for Greek letter organizations, and providing security services for off-campus chapter houses) might imply that the institution had assumed a duty of supervision.

Given that the mere existence of an institutional policy creates the potential for liability on the grounds of duty, institutions may not want to implement appropriate policies. If *Furek* applied in all jurisdictions, it would be better from a legal perspective for institutions to leave Greek organizations to their own devices and to hand hazing prevention over to the organizations' international or national headquarters (Paine, 1994). Even in those jurisdictions where *Furek* is law, however, educational institutions have legal and ethical responsibilities not only to have an antihazing policy but also to enforce it. The policy would ostensibly protect Greeks, as well as the rest of the student body. This bind between the obligation to have a policy and the dangers of that policy underscores the stark contrast between a higher education institution and an industrial corporation in making decisions and policies that affect liability. In the context of a university or college, the safety of students should take precedence over liability analysis. Since the safety of students is of paramount importance, it is sometimes necessary to have a policy protecting them from certain activities that might expose them to liability if not properly performed. However, if the institution is attentive to and enforces the policies it has set forth for the protection of its students, not only is it in a better liability position, but it is also fulfilling its ethical duty toward its students.

If students become injured while engaging in activities that institutions have not chosen to supervise or control, and if students then make a charge of negligence, courts have refused to hold institutions or Greek letter organizations liable. This was true, for instance, in *Whitlock v. University of Denver,* 744 P.2d 54 (Colo. 1987) and *Millard v. Osborne,* 611 A.2d 715 (Pa. Super. Ct. 1992). Whitlock was injured on a trampoline in the yard of his fraternity house, which was on land leased from the university. The court found no special relationship based on Whitlock's status as a student or on the lessor-lessee status that the university had with the fraternity. Therefore, the university was found to have had no duty to supervise and control such activities.

Furthermore, when students are injured during social events sponsored by Greek letter organizations because these students have voluntarily and intentionally engaged in the conduct leading to the injury, they have generally not succeeded in actions against the organizations or institutions. For example, in *Foster v. Purdue University,* 567 N.E.2d 865 (Ind. Ct. App. 1991), a fraternity member was unsuccessful in alleging negligence against his chapter for maintaining a water slide during a philanthropic event. The student had intentionally and voluntarily dived headfirst onto the slide and had been rendered a quadriplegic. When the injury results from misconduct by other Greek letter organization members, however, both the individual member and the organization might be found liable (Kaplin and Lee, 1995).

If the institution clearly articulates its expectations about the behavior of Greek letter organization members, it may deter misconduct. Because there is potential for greater institutional liability with more extensive regulation, some institutions recognize fraternities and sororities with statements similar to those used to recognize other student organizations. These statements outline the institution's regulations and, among other things, elicit the Greek letter organization's assurance that it will obtain insurance coverage, adhere to fire and building codes, and comply with the institution's policy on serving alcohol. Such statements may, however, limit the institution's authority to regulate the Greek letter organization's activities, although individual members can still be disciplined for violating student codes or regulations (Kaplin and Lee, 1995).

Hazing

Forty states have enacted statutes making hazing illegal; all but three of those laws have been passed since 1978. Hazing participants can now be charged with simple or aggravated assault or battery, kidnapping, false imprisonment, manslaughter, or even murder (Richmond, 1989). This legislation was prompted by injuries and deaths resulting from hazing injuries. Despite these criminal statutes, strong policies by institutions and organizational headquarters, and educational efforts against hazing, the practice persists in Greek letter organizations.

Legal definitions of hazing employed by courts are connected to state statutes, and thus may vary. However, the lack of a common definition of hazing should not deter an institution from moving toward an enforceable policy prohibiting such conduct. Senior student affairs officers should develop an institutional policy defining and prohibiting hazing that is sufficiently broad to prohibit behaviors and activities including

- Actions that recklessly or intentionally endanger students' safety or their physical or mental health
- Forced or required consumption of any food, liquor, drug, or other substance
- Forced participation in physical activities, such as calisthenics, exercises, or so-called games
- Exposure to the elements
- Excessive fatigue resulting from sleep deprivation, physical activities, or exercise
- Physical brutality, including paddling, branding, and striking with fists, open hands, or objects
- Verbal abuse, including "lineups" and berating of individuals

- Forced or required conduct that could embarrass or negatively affect the individual's dignity, including the wearing of apparel that is conspicuous or extraordinary and the performance of public stunts and activities
- Denial of sufficient time to study
- Assignment of activities that are illegal or unlawful or that might be morally offensive to individual pledges
- Forced trips that involve kidnapping or stranding individuals
- The intentional creation of cleanup work or labor (Richmond, 1987)

Hazing continues to cause human tragedies, administrative problems, and legal nightmares for institutions, chapters, and individuals.

According to those who advocate greater punishments for hazing, society continues to blame the victims for being involved in the situations in the first place and does not punish the true perpetrators—either individuals or chapters—strongly enough (Gose, 1997). Some states treat hazing as a felony if serious injury or death results, but most only classify it as a criminal misdemeanor (Richmond, 1989).

Forty-seven people died as a result of hazing incidents between 1973 and 1996. Some believe that the numbers are actually substantially higher, as many cases of hazing either go unreported or are classified as other types of offenses (Franta, 1996–1997).

Some universities are taking hazing more seriously now than in the past. Texas A&M says it will no longer keep hazing investigations confidential, which it did until this year. "Now, we're going to make sure that every time this happens, people know about it," said Mary Jo Powell, a university spokeswoman (Gose, 1997, p. A37).

Some state hazing statutes extend criminal liability to people who knowingly permit, fail to report, or acquiesce in hazing. That implicates faculty and administrative or advisory staff who work with Greek letter organizations (Curry, 1989). As penalties for violating the statutes, including failing to report or participating passively, people can be fined or even incarcerated. In states with such statutes, senior student affairs officers and administrative staff should be particularly aware of those laws and of hazing activities on their campuses.

In addition to these legal consequences, institutions could be liable if hazing causes injuries to students or others. These tort claims (for example, of negligence) would come on top of the criminal claims brought by the state (Curry, 1989). Those who fail to understand and respond to all of these legal implications through appropriate education and training risk their individual reputations and finances, as well as those of their students and institutions.

Senior student affairs officers should also keep in mind that the *Furek* case demonstrates a growing tendency toward holding institutions liable for students' actions, even when those actions are realistically outside the institution's control. Thus, institutions have devised two strategies for dealing with Greek hazing: (1) exercise very strict control over Greek letter organizations and (2) exercise no control at all. With control, of course, comes legal responsibility.

Yet, on the continuum of degrees of institutional control, those schools willing to exercise only partial control over their Greek letter organizations assume the greater risk of liability. For this reason, many institutions are now either choosing between the two extremes of strict policing or they are disassociating themselves from Greek letter organizations (Curry, 1989). Dissociation means that the institution does not recognize student membership in fraternities and sororities. These groups would be operating outside the jurisdiction of the college or university. In addition, the institution will indicate that it has no Greek letter organizations on campus. Even a dissociated university or college still possesses a vested interest in the welfare of its students, however. A Greek system that is not recognized by the university then does not have access to campus advising and resources. Thus, the opportunities for improvement are considerably lessened, and the system may deteriorate further (Curry, 1989).

Senior student affairs officers must therefore provide educational programs about hazing for those rushing an organization and for new and initiated members. In addition, administrators must hold groups accountable for hazing violations. Finally, they need to review policies and procedures relating to Greek letter organizations every year. Incidents stemming from alcohol abuse and hazing should not be tolerated. The days of giving a fraternity or sorority "another chance" are quickly coming to an end. Many institutions and national and international Greek organizations are simply suspending the operations of groups that fail to heed this message and the call to become active members of an academic community.

Alcohol

Given the high incidence of alcohol use among college students in general, and among members of Greek letter organizations in particular (see discussion in Chapter Five), it is understandable that institutions have serious liability concerns. An insurer of a national fraternity performed a survey of claims between 1987 and 1991. The survey linked alcohol abuse to 86 percent of fatalities, 86 percent of injuries resulting in paralysis, 72 percent of serious injuries, 88 percent of psychological injuries, and 97 percent of reported cases of sexual assault (Harris and Harris of Kentucky, 1996). Of the claims relating to alcohol use, more than 61 percent involved underage drinking (Harris and Harris of Kentucky, 1996). Finally, according to a study released by the Mayo Clinic, alcohol is currently linked to 97 percent of all investigated hazing incidents (Franta, 1996–1997).

An increasing number of incidents resulting in serious injury or death underscore the seriousness of the binge drinking issue. Recently, an underage student at Louisiana State University died of alcohol poisoning from binge drinking after celebrating a bid to join a fraternity. His blood alcohol level was more than six times the legal limit of intoxication for automobile drivers (Henry, 1997). Over the past year alone, several fraternities have been suspended and sued over deaths linked to alcohol. In one case, the national headquarters of a fraternity suspended a University of California-Los Angeles chapter after two members drowned in a lake at a social function involving alcohol; these deaths resulted in criminal charges. Eight members of a Maryland fraternity were charged with manslaughter after an alcohol-poisoning death. In Potsdam, New York, eight fraternity members pleaded guilty in the hazing death of a seventeen-year-old new member who choked on his own vomit after drinking excessive amounts of alcohol (Peterson and Marshall, 1997).

These figures and the problems they represent have strong ramifications for chief student affairs officers and institutions. Notwithstanding institutions' efforts to decrease student drinking, institutional officials often feel overwhelmed and helpless when attempting to enforce underage drinking restrictions (Stewart, 1988).

The national headquarters of a number of fraternities are taking action against excessive alcohol consumption on campus and have asked senior student affairs officers for their cooperation in these efforts. Some organizations have made bold but seemingly necessary commitments. For example, Sigma Nu and Phi Delta Theta fraternities have each pledged that by the year 2000, every one of its chapters will have alcohol-free and substance-free facilities or they will not continue to exist as a chartered group of that fraternity (Henry, 1997). This means that all their chapters that have facilities will ban alcohol and other drugs from their premises. In April 1997, the National Interfraternity Conference chose five campuses to test a new Greek standards program entitled "Select 2000," which included a ban on alcohol. Some universities have already acted to ban alcohol on campus, including fraternity houses (Chorley, 1997); others are moving in that direction.

State legislatures continue to create laws that make Greek organizations increasingly liable for personal injury resulting from alcohol-related activity (Bickel, 1996). A growing number of states have social host liability statutes that impose a legal duty on those who provide alcohol to an intoxicated person; the provider becomes responsible to third parties for the negligent acts of the intoxicated person (Kaplin and Lee, 1995). These statutes give a private host, such as a Greek letter organization, the duties that have long existed for those who operate public establishments in which alcohol is served.

The rise of social host liability statutes and theories imperils Greek organizations and could eventually become a major liability concern for institutions, as well. For instance, in *Estate of Hernandez v. Arizona Board of Regents,* 866 P.2d 1330 (Ariz. 1994), Hernandez died after a car accident that initially left him a blind, brain-damaged quadriplegic. The driver of the vehicle that struck him was an underage new member of a Greek letter organization and had become extremely intoxicated at a chapter party. Hernandez's estate sued the driver, the university, national and local chapters, the house corporation (the alumni organization that oversees the facility and, in some cases, the property and that is ultimately responsible for the financial operation), and each member of the chapter that contributed money to the social fund used to purchase the alcohol (Powell, 1995). Although the university settled the claims it faced out of court and was dropped from the lawsuit, the plaintiff's argument was that the university was negligent in continuing to lease the house to the house corporation when it knew the organization served alcohol to underage students (Kaplin and Lee, 1995). The Arizona Supreme Court held that the Greek organization was obligated to avoid furnishing alcohol to underage consumers. Although institutions are not generally deemed social hosts, they may face future attempts to assert that they are liable in this way for their alleged obligations with respect to Greek letter organizations.

Institutions have incorporated tough policies on alcohol use, but apparently there has been no corresponding decrease in institutional exposure to either lawsuits or liability for resulting injuries (Paine, 1994). In fact, as with general tort liability, an institution's increased regulation and control of student drinking may actually increase its exposure to liability. A court may view the regulation as evidence that the institution has assumed a duty. This can provide grounds for a negligence action based on improper exercise of a duty (Paine, 1994).

Kaplin and Lee (1995) believe that institutions may safely rely on *Bradshaw* in connection with liability situations involving alcohol, insofar as it failed to find a custodial relationship between the institution and its students. With regulations on drinking that go beyond state law, however, institutions could be found liable for failing to perform their duty reasonably if (1) the regulations are interpreted as the voluntary assumption of specific custodial duties regarding alcohol and (2) institutions make an insufficient attempt to enforce them. As with hazing regulations, given the mission of higher education institutions, it seems necessary to have *and* to enforce alcohol regulations for the safety and betterment of students. Institutions' legal counsel should, however, review any proposed policies regarding alcohol use.

Sexual Assault

Some studies have shown that a female's chance of being sexually assaulted as a college student is 20 to 25 percent; first-year female students are at the greatest risk. At fraternity parties and other events, male Greek members often engage in sexual misbehavior, which occasionally includes sexual assault, (Fossey and Smith, 1995).

Federal laws, such as the Ramstad Amendment and the Student Right-to-Know and Campus Security Act (hereafter referred to as the Campus Security Act), have assigned colleges and universities more responsibility for preventing sexual assaults. The Ramstad Amendment requires institutions to adopt policies to prevent sex offenses, as well as procedures to deal with such offenses when they occur, including institutional sanctions. The Campus Security Act requires institutions to gather information about crimes that occur on their campuses and to make that information available to the public. By obligating institutions to warn students of possible crimes, this legislation may increase an institution's exposure to liability.

Liability for sexual assaults on campus depends on whether institutions are considered to have a special relationship with students and whether the institution breached that relationship. Institutions have a duty to caution students against foreseeable dangers. They also owe students and employees a reasonably safe environment in which to live and work (Fossey and Smith, 1995).

If an institution breaches its duty by failing to provide adequate security or warnings and then an assault occurs on campus, an institution could be held liable for monetary damages. This happened, for example, in *Peterson* v. *San Francisco Community College District,* 685 P.2d 1193 (Cal. 1992). A student sustained injuries as a result of an attempted rape in the institution's parking lot. The plaintiff alleged that the college should have foreseen that this type of incident could occur because there had been prior sexual assault attempts in that parking lot. Peterson alleged that the institution had failed to warn adequately students of the potential danger and had failed to trim the foliage around the parking lot, thereby increasing the possibility of such an assault. The college was found liable.

Other cases have found that, because an institution of higher education has a high concentration of young people, it has a greater duty than other types of organizations to provide safe conditions. The court drew this conclusion in *Mullins* v. *Pine Manor College,* 449 N.E.2d 331 (Mass. 1983): "The concentration of young people, especially young women, on a college campus, creates favorable opportunities for criminal behavior. The threat of criminal acts of third parties to resident students is self-evident, and the college is the party which is in the position to take those steps which are necessary to ensure the safety of its students."

One court, however, refused to find such a duty when the alleged rape did not occur at a university-sponsored activity. In *Leonardi* v. *Bradley University,* 625 N.E.2d 431 (Ill. Ct. App. 1983), the Illinois Court of Appeals found that whereas the institution might owe a higher duty of care to students involved in university-sponsored activities, a late-night visit to a fraternity house did not qualify as such an activity. The court reasoned that students involved in university-sponsored activities were of the legal designation known as *business invitees,* which carries with it a particular standard of care. Furthermore, the court argued that participation in nonsponsored activities, such as Greek parties, did not raise an injured student's status to that legal status and elevated standard of care.

Institutional Policies to Regulate Greek Organizations

An Internet search on the topic of *university policies for Greek organizations* yielded more than 10,590,025 matches. Clearly, there is a significant amount of institutional regulation of the Greek system. The extent of regulation that institutions exert over Greeks varies, however. "About a third of America's colleges exercise control over [Greek letter organizations]. The remainder maintain greater distance, including a third that treat them as completely independent entities"

(Pavela, 1995, p. 489). This diversity of approaches results from varying law and policy perspectives across the country.

From a strictly legal perspective, it is better for universities to maintain distance from any entity, including Greek letter organizations. Greek letter organizations are an integral part of many institutions, though, and maintaining such a distance can be problematic. An institution can face liability for exercising either too much or too little control over students (Pavela, 1995). As a result, an institution's decision about how it regulates Greek letter organizations must be a matter of organizational choice. An institution may find some or all of the following policies to be appropriate for its purposes in dealing with Greek letter organizations on campus and legal issues.

Relationship Statements. Such statements could include a description of the limited purpose of recognition; acknowledgment that the Greek letter organization is independently chartered; confirmation that the college assumes no responsibility for supervision, control, safety, security, or other services with respect to the Greek letter organization; and a requirement that the Greek letter organization furnish evidence that it carries sufficient insurance to cover its risks (Gulland and Powell, 1989). Although the existence of such a recognition statement might defeat a claim that the institution has assumed a duty to supervise Greek letter organization members, it might also limit the institution's authority to regulate the organization's activities (Kaplin and Lee, 1995).

Chapter Seven of this volume describes a program, *Greek Life: A Foundation for the Future,* that the University of Maryland at College Park implemented to reform its Greek system. The plan proposed the elimination of pledging, required personal development programs, active chapter advisers, an internal judicial system, live-in house directors, and chapter management plans with annual reports on this plan's success (Pavela, 1995).

A comprehensive program such as this poses two significant potential legal problems. First, as previously discussed, greater institutional control could result in greater liability. Second, a program such as Maryland's might be subject to challenge as an unlawful interference with students' rights to freedom of association. In *Healy* v. *James,* 408 U.S. 169 (1972), the Supreme Court found that students have a right to form and operate organizations without institutional interference; in other words, students have a fundamental freedom of association. Plans such as Maryland's arguably place too many restrictions and requirements on students' rights. To date, however, Maryland's plan has not been challenged, and the program has exceeded the university's expectations for improving the system (D. Bagwell, personal communication, April 1997).

Even if a plan such as Maryland's were challenged, however, it might be upheld. In *Healy,* (now Chief) Justice Rehnquist stated, "The government as employer or school administrator may impose upon employees and students reasonable regulations that would be impermissible if imposed by the government upon all citizens." Citing *Esteban* v. *Central Missouri State College,* 415 F.2d

1077 (1969), Rehnquist argued that an institution "may expect that its students adhere to generally accepted standards of conduct" (*Healy v. James,* 408 U.S. 169 [1972]).

Apparently, if regulations policies are fair, not arbitrary or punitive, an institution could reasonably require students "in a broad range of leadership positions [and affiliated groups] to demonstrate special academic proficiency, undertake leadership training, and serve as role models for their peers" (Pavela, 1995). Although the precedent is not definitive, then, an institution could implement greater control via policy statements without impinging on a student's right to freedom of association.

Hazing. Higher education institutions have adopted policies that reflect or incorporate applicable state statutes into institutional policy (Buchanon, Shanley, Correnti, and Hammond, 1982). State statutes vary, however, and as such, it can be problematic if the statute is too vague to direct student behavior explicitly.

An institutional hazing policy should be specific enough to provide appropriate direction. At a minimum, the behaviors and activities listed in the earlier section on hazing should be prohibited. The policy should prohibit coerced activities and behaviors and should reflect that the rules apply to all members (active or alumni), guests, and new members.

An institution should reconcile its applicable state statute with the above suggestions and determine which, if any, are included in the statute. If they are not, a decision should be made as to whether it would be beneficial to include them in the institution's hazing policy.

Alcohol. Having an appropriate policy regarding alcohol use is important from a legal perspective (Buchanon, 1983), even though studies have shown that institutional alcohol policies have little impact on students' drinking patterns (Hanson and Engs, 1995).

An institutional alcohol policy should, at a minimum, reflect local, state, and federal law and should also reflect an institution's expectations about alcohol use (Buchanon, 1983). Institutional rules on alcohol use should be reasonable and enforceable. Adopting such rules creates a duty to enforce them, and once such a duty is assumed, failure to enforce rules properly could be construed as negligence (Smith, 1989). Some possible provisions to include in an alcohol policy include prohibitions on alcohol use by minors, prohibitions regarding the use of kegs and other alcohol containers, limitations on where alcohol may be consumed, and initiatives that encourage students of legal age to "bring their own" and use third-party vendors.

Another aspect of an alcohol policy that could help reduce liability is if it assigns responsibility to students and their hosts for complying with state and federal laws (see, for example, *Millard v. Osborne* at 717). In *Millard,* the court found that because the institution's handbook accorded responsibility to the student's hosts, the institution was absolved of liability. This absolution came despite evidence that the school did enforce its own alcohol regulations and that it did not do so consistently.

Sexual Assault. A comprehensive policy and education program should reduce an institution's exposure to liability for sexual assaults to its students. According to Walton (1994), the policy should

- Be publicized
- Clearly define institutional philosophy
- Describe a plan for managing sexual assaults
- Include procedures for the student's report of the assault, the institutional investigation, a referral to law enforcement authorities, an announcement to the community, and the institutional judicial process
- Be flexible enough to provide for all situations
- Be formulated to protect the privacy, confidentiality, and civil rights of victims and alleged attackers
- Comply with the Campus Security Act

Hearings about sexual assaults should be handled by the institution's judicial process, not a Greek judicial board, because of the sensitive and serious nature of such incidents. Institutions should also immediately contact legal counsel and refer the matter to appropriate law enforcement officials (Walton, 1994).

Social Events or Parties. Policies regarding social events are closely related to alcohol policies. Like alcohol policies, they should be reasonable and enforceable. Special attention should be given to the responsibilities placed on the student. In *Booker* v. *Lehigh University,* 800 F. Supp. 234 (E.D. Pa 1992) aff'd 995 F.2d 215 (3rd Cir. 1993), an underage student was seriously injured after she had been drinking at on-campus Greek-sponsored events and then fell. The plaintiff alleged that the institution was liable because it had breached a duty created by its social event policy. Lehigh's social policy required party hosts to register the event with the institution and to hire a security guard to check identification. The policy, however, explicitly described and emphasized the host's responsibilities to prevent underage drinking. The court rejected the in loco parentis argument and decided in favor of the institution.

Social event policies can include such requirements as that the host organization must register the event with the institution or sign a social event contract. Social event contracts can include a variety of obligations for hosts, such as checking identification at the door, providing names of chapter individuals who will be responsible for ensuring compliance with laws and policies, and requiring third-party vendors for alcohol. Some institutions require Greek organizations to ensure that event hosts serve adequate alternatives to alcoholic beverages, as well as specified amounts of food that is not salty. Requirements such as these are often included in the Greeks' own risk management policies, which their national headquarters have set forth.

Some institutions use peer monitoring boards, or "party patrols," to enforce social event policies. These peer monitors are members of Greek letter organizations who, on a rotating basis, serve as enforcement officials of institutional or self-governing social event policies. In a systemwide move that has proven controversial among the various women's Greek organizations, the National Panhellenic Conference in fall 1996 adopted a resolution that advised its member groups to refrain from acting as social event peer monitors and urged them to resist institutional personnel's pressure to serve as such. Campus Greek affairs professionals by and large believe, however, that peer monitoring groups are appropriate. Although this practice may raise some liability concerns, these concerns are outweighed by the opportunity to ensure a safe environment for students.

Considering Institutional Policies. The following list is not meant to be exhaustive, but it includes policies that institutions could consider when responding to legal liability issues regarding Greek letter organizations. Campus administrators would be wise to have these policies in place before any liability issues occur. All of these policies would apply to Greek letter organizations, and some would extend to all recognized student organizations:

• Alcohol
• Hazing
• Social event peer monitoring
• Sexual assault
• Auxiliary organizations (such as "little sisters" and "little brothers")
• Discrimination or harassment
• Free or protected speech
• Student conduct
• Academic honesty
• Distribution of guidelines (where and what may be posted)
• Technology and cyberspace
• Raffles and lotteries

The legal ramifications of hosting Greek letter organizations continue to evolve. It is clear that a lack of basic knowledge or awareness of potential liability pitfalls is no longer a viable option for senior student affairs officers. If institutions are to realize any benefit from having Greek letter organizations on their campuses, they must provide students with positive learning opportunities. This requires the institution, Greek organizations, national and international headquarters, and individual members to work together to understand the institution's mission and incorporate it into their regular activities. The common goal should be to manage, reduce, and even eliminate risks posed by activities and behavior and to try achieving the fraternal ideals on which the organizations were founded. True Greek learning communities can exist if members work toward this important goal.

References

Astin, A. W. *What Matters in College? Four Critical Years Revisited.* San Francisco: Jossey-Bass, 1993.

Bickel, R. Unpublished outline for group discussion on issues of Greek life. Circulated at a conference at the University of Montana, 1996.

Buchanon, E. "Alcohol on Campus and Possible Liability." *NASPA Journal,* 1983, *21,* 2–19.

Buchanon, E., Shanley, M., Correnti, P., and Hammond, E. "Hazing: Collective Stupidity, Insensitivity, and Irresponsibility." *NASPA Journal,* 1982, *20,* 56–68.

Chorley, K. "IFC Beats the UI in the Race to Go Dry." *The Daily Iowan,* Oct. 28, 1997, p. 1A.

Curry, S. "Hazing and the 'Rush' Toward Reform: Responses from Universities, Fraternities, State Legislatures, and the Courts." *Journal of College and University Law,* 1989, *16,* 93–117.

Fossey, R., and Smith, M. "Institutional Liability for Campus Rapes: The Emerging Law." *Journal of Law and Education,* 1995, *24,* 377–401.

Franta, D. "Cain Slew Abel: Hazing—The Fratricide of Brotherhood." *Journal of Kappa Alpha,* Winter 1996–1997, pp. 5–9.

Gose, B. "Efforts to End Fraternity Hazing Said to Have Largely Failed: Critics Say State Laws Have Been Ineffective, in Part Because of a Tendency to Blame the Victims." *Chronicle of Higher Education,* Apr. 18, 1997, pp. A37–A38.

Gulland, D., and Powell, M. *Colleges, Fraternities and Sororities.* A White Paper on Tort Liability Issues. Washington, D.C.: American Council on Education, 1989.

Hanson, D. J., and Engs, R. C. "Collegiate Drinking: Administrator Perception, Campus Policies, and Student Behaviors." *NASPA Journal,* 1995, *32* (2), 106–114.

Harris and Harris of Kentucky. *Fraternity Claims Analysis, 1987–1995.* (3rd ed.) Louisville: Harris and Harris of Kentucky, 1996.

Henry, T. "Drinking Death Deals a Blow to College Efforts." *USA Today,* Aug. 28, 1997, p. D–1.

Kaplin, W. A., and Lee, B. A. *The Law of Higher Education: A Comprehensive Guide to Legal Implications of Administrative Decision Making.* (3rd ed.) San Francisco: Jossey-Bass, 1995.

Kuh, G. D. "Guiding Principles for Creating Seamless Learning Environments for Undergraduates." *Journal of College Student Development,* 1996, *37* (2), 135–148.

Kuh, G. D., Pascarella, E. T., and Wechsler, H. "The Questionable Value of Fraternities." *Chronicle of Higher Education,* 1996, *43* (4), A68.

Maisel, J. P. "Social Fraternities and Sororities Are Not Conducive to the Educational Process." *NASPA Journal,* 1990, *28* (1), 8–12.

Paine, E. "Recent Trends in Fraternity-Related Liability." *Journal of Law and Education,* 1994, *23,* 191–210.

Pascarella, E. T., and Terenzini, P. T. *How College Affects Students: Findings and Insights from Twenty Years of Research.* San Francisco: Jossey-Bass, 1991.

Pavela, G. "Regulating Fraternities." *Synthesis: Law and Policy in Higher Education,* 1995, *7,* 489–508.

Peterson, R., and Marshall, S. "Louisiana Officials to Investigate Binge-Drinking Death." *USA Today,* Aug. 28, 1997, p. 3–A.

Powell, G. "Arizona Court: Fraternities Are Drinking Clubs." *Fraternal Law,* 1995, *53,* 1–2.

Richmond, D. R. "The Legal Implications of Fraternity Hazing." *NASPA Journal,* 1989, *26* (4), 300–307.

Richmond, R. "Putting an End to Fraternity Hazing." *NASPA Journal,* 1987, *24,* 48–52.

Smith, M. "Students, Suds, and Summonses: Strategies for Coping with Campus Alcohol Abuse." *Journal of College Student Development,* 1989, *30,* 118–122.

Stewart, G. "Social Host Liability on Campus: Taking the 'High' out of Higher Education." *Dickinson Law Review,* 1988, *92,* 665.

Terenzini, P. T., Pascarella, E. T., and Blimling, G. S. "Students' Out-of-Class Experiences and Their Influence on Learning and Cognitive Development: A Literature Review." *Journal of College Student Development*, 1996, *37* (2), 149–162.

Walton, S. "Date Rape: New Liability for Colleges and Universities?" *NASPA Journal*, 1994, *31*, 195–200.

Wechsler, H. "Alcohol and the American College Campus: A Report from the Harvard School of Public Health." *Change*, July–Aug. 1996, pp. 20–60.

NICHOLAS J. HENNESSY is completing his doctorate in higher education administration at Bowling Green State University in Bowling Green, Ohio. An attorney, he practiced commercial litigation in Florida before coming to Bowling Green.

LISA M. HUSON is general counsel for Eastern Illinois University. Prior to her employment there, she was an assistant attorney general for the state of Kansas.

Greek letter organizations continue to face the challenge of closing the gap between the high standards they profess to espouse and the inappropriate behaviors of their members. Resources are available, however, to help senior student affairs officers and Greek members develop standards and expectations for chapters.

Standards and Expectations for Greek Letter Organizations

Michael D. Shonrock

As the twenty-first century approaches, "colleges and universities must ensure that fraternity members live up to the standards expected of all students and the standards that fraternities themselves espouse. When groups or individuals fail to meet these goals, administrators and fraternity leaders must act decisively to stem further abuse and reaffirm the institution's overarching educational mission" (Kuh, Pascarella, and Wechsler, 1996, p. A68). Campus administrators must work with Greek letter organizations to help them understand the core values of the institution. These core values must in some fashion be reflected in institution policies governing such areas as behavior and other kinds of expectations or standards. Senior student affairs officers then must hold fraternities and sororities accountable for their actions.

Since the origin of fraternities and sororities in the eighteenth century, Greeks have asserted a commitment to standards of "high ideals and high moral and ethical teachings . . . [and] to the high purposes of the group and of the responsibility which membership requires" (Anson and Marchesani, 1991, pp. 1–13). Unfortunately, membership behavior today does not reflect those ideals and purposes. Abusing alcohol, performing poorly in classes, and hazing are just a few of the problems that Greek letter organizations have not been able to confront and resolve successfully.

The challenge for Greek letter organizations is to resolve the conflict between the values they espouse and the inappropriate behavior in which some members engage. Many institutions have standards and expectations for their student organizations, including fraternities and sororities. These standards most often take the form of student codes of conduct that outline acceptable behaviors for students and policies and procedures for student organizations' operations.

Because of persistent problems with Greek students' behavior, many institutions and Greek organization headquarters have developed additional policies just for dealing with Greek chapters. These policies go a step further than student codes of conduct or policies and procedures for other student organizations. In general terms, they set benchmarks for what constitutes the acceptable operation of a Greek letter organization, including behavior, academic performance, alumni relations, and so on.

The purpose of this chapter is to describe the challenging process of developing and implementing standards for Greek organizations. The chapter provides examples of policy statements and codes of standards and expectations from institutions of higher education, Greek organizations, and student affairs associations.

Institutional Standards and Expectations

In the 1990s, because Greek letter organizations were not resolving such issues as hazing, alcohol abuse, and other negative behavior, many colleges and universities established commissions such *The Miami Model for Greek Excellence* at Miami University and *Greek Life: A Foundation for the Future* at the University of Maryland at College Park. These commissions were intended to define clearly the institutions' relationship with, and expectations of, Greek organizations.

Greek Life, Maryland's comprehensive plan, recognized that standards already exist in the charters, constitutions, and bylaws of fraternities and sororities. Drury Bagwell, associate vice chancellor for student affairs at the University of Maryland at College Park stated,

> Before writing *Greek Life* we went back to all of our nationals on campus and looked at what they say they exist for. Then we developed a game plan that tries to meet those purposes. At the core of this are two very important features: (1) we're trying to change the culture without wiping out the system; and (2) we're trying to change the package so students who would be interested in joining are the kinds of people who would do community service, focus on scholarship, want to bond with others in a constructive way, and develop lasting ties with the institution. [Pavela, 1995b, p. 493]

The standards and expectations of *Greek Life* were intended to complement the institution's larger mission and help Greek organizations realize the ideals expressed in their rituals. Performance standards of *Greek Life* include membership development, chapter development, chapter outreach, and chapter facility management. For example, the membership development standards relate to academic achievement, concerns about the poor performance of first-year students and the idea of deferred rush, and the education of new members. In addition, the lengthy pledge period as practiced today would be abolished to minimize hazing opportunities (Pavela, 1996).

Overall, *Greek Life* recognizes that "the high ideals of scholarship, friendship, leadership and service, among other principles, can be realized by the implementation of the standards" (Pavela, 1995a, pp. 506–507). As institutions attempt to create learning communities within their campus environments, plans such as Maryland's are important models. Such plans can help fraternities and sororities align themselves more closely with the institution's educational mission and values and give institutions mechanisms to ensure this alignment. These plans also establish standards and expectations by which organizations can operate, and they describe processes for creating such plans that can be adapted to other institutions.

Greek Headquarters' Standards and Expectations

Fraternity and sorority headquarters have also developed comprehensive standards and minimum expectations (Gose, 1997). These standards and expectations address alumni relations, chapter operations, codes of conduct, community involvement, financial management, fraternity education, facilities, rules, membership, risk management, ritual, and scholarship.

One example, Sigma Alpha Epsilon's *Standards of Excellence,* states, "Greek organizations have a special obligation and opportunity to contribute to the quality of campus life. Their long history on many campuses, their national structure and network, and the significant number of students they involve make it potentially possible for them to make a positive contribution to student life. Rigorous accountability to their institution and to the national organizations and strenuous self-regulation are required to enable sororities and fraternities to realize their potential as a positive force" (Sigma Alpha Epsilon Fraternity, 1996, p. 1).

In response to continuing problems with alcohol use, hazing, and other safety issues, some national and international offices have adopted the Fraternity Insurance Purchasing Group (FIPG) risk management policy. This policy prescribes specific standards and expectations regarding alcohol and drugs, hazing, sexual abuse and harassment, fire and health safety, and education. For example, the FIPG policy on sexual abuse and harassment states, "The fraternity will not tolerate or condone any form of sexist or sexually abusive behavior on the part of its members, whether physical, mental or emotional" (Fraternity Insurance Purchasing Group, 1996).

Senior student affairs officers can also work with students and alumni to understand these standards and expectations. They should realize that fraternity and sorority leaders have access to chapter bylaws, constitutions, and rituals, which provide the foundation for chapter standards and membership expectations. Although the ritual is secret in most fraternities and sororities, the bylaws and constitutions are available and printed in various headquarters' handbooks and publications (Anson and Marchesani, 1991). If senior student affairs officers are aware of these resources and obtain copies of them, they can help Greek letter organizations establish reasonable standards and expectations.

Student Affairs Association Standards

Student affairs administrators, through professional associations, have developed important standards and expectations for working with various student affairs programs, including Greek letter organizations.

CAS Standards. Standards for handling Greek affairs have been designed specifically for student affairs staff. In 1979, the Council for the Advancement of Standards (CAS) was formed with assistance from the American College Personnel Association and the National Association of Student Personnel Administrators. The intention was to establish, disseminate, and advocate professional standards and guidelines on a nationwide basis for student services programs and services (Council for the Advancement of Standards, 1997; Lange, 1986). These standards and expectations apply to a wide range of such programs, including Greek advising. The CAS standards offer a vehicle for institution program assessment, thereby allowing student affairs staff to evaluate more quickly. In addition, the assessment can be conducted in a less threatening manner than if it came from outside (Lange, 1986).

CAS has produced two documents associated with their standards—*Fraternity and Sorority Advising: Self-Assessment Guide* (Council for the Advancement of Standards, 1992) and *Standards and Guidelines for Fraternity and Sorority Advising* (Council for the Advancement of Standards, 1997). Both are relevant to senior student affairs staff interested in working with Greeks to establish standards consistent with learning communities.

Fraternity and Sorority Advising: Self-Assessment Guide is divided into thirteen parts: mission, program, leadership and management, organization and administration, human resources, funding, facilities, legal responsibilities, equal opportunity and affirmative action, campus and community relations, multicultural programs and services, ethics, and evaluation. It identifies noncompliance or compliance with specific assessment criteria. For example, CAS assessment criteria for advising an institution's Greek life program include evaluating the purpose, organization, focus on student development, educational programming, relationship with the institution, membership development, advising, and outcomes. *Standards and Guidelines for Fraternity and Sorority Advising* identifies the institutional support necessary to ensure compliance with the assessment criteria for fraternities and sororities.

Joint Statement on Rights and Freedoms. As senior student affairs officers try to establish standards for Greek letter organizations, the *Joint Statement on Rights and Freedoms of Students* (Mullendore, 1992) may also be helpful. The *Joint Statement* articulates a set of standards recognized by student affairs practitioners promoting freedom of association and conduct expectations. The *Joint Statement* advocates that students be responsible for the following things: their academic growth, active participation in institutional policy development, the consequences of their decisions, and commitment to behavior that has a positive influence on the campus community (Mullendore and Bryan, 1992).

The *Joint Statement* notes that institutions might choose to require student organizations (including fraternities and sororities) to submit a statement of purpose; criteria for membership; rules and procedures; and commitment to nondiscrimination on the basis of race, creed, or national origin. Students affiliated with fraternities and sororities are both residents of the United States and members of the academic community. As citizens, students should enjoy the same freedom of speech, peaceful assembly, and right of petition that other citizens enjoy. As members of the academic community, they are subject to the obligations that come with this membership (Mullendore, 1992). In this regard, the *Joint Statement* promotes self-assessment within fraternities and sororities.

Reasonable Expectations. Another resource for senior student affairs administrators in developing standards and expectations for use with Greek letter organizations is *Reasonable Expectations* (National Association of Student Personnel Administrators, 1996). In establishing standards and expectations for fraternities and sororities, this document provides a conceptual framework for senior student affairs officers. *Reasonable Expectations* states that just as students have certain expectations of their institutions, the institutions have expectations of their students. The goal of the document is to encourage administrators, faculty, staff, and students to help develop environments in which learning can take place. It emphasizes that everyone invested in student learning has a responsibility to work toward this goal.

Accountability and Empowerment. These documents can help senior student affairs officers develop standards and expectations with, and for, fraternity and sorority chapters. No one document provides all the information needed to establish effective standards and expectations for Greek letter organizations. Each, however, emphasizes the responsibility of the student as a member of a learning community.

The challenge of establishing standards and expectations for Greek letter organizations is complicated by the recognition that "people today, and college-age students in particular, are having a very difficult time holding each other accountable. Greek chapters certainly need to do a better job and all of us need to do a better job [in this regard] teaching them how" (R. L. Orians, executive director, Pi Kappa Alpha fraternity, personal communication, Nov. 12, 1996). It is essential that student affairs administrators articulate to fraternity and sorority members the importance of confrontation. This confrontation, however, should be positive. Learning communities are built on a foundation of strong relationships. These relationships are characterized by active communication, which involves confronting others and helping them understand what is expected of them in terms of behavioral expectations and other standards.

Perhaps the underlying philosophy for senior student affairs officers to adopt here is one of empowerment. Students support that which they help create and that for which they have responsibility. This philosophy must guide any and all development of standards and expectations for Greek letter organizations. These standards and expectations must be established by a partnership of college and university student affairs professionals, faculty, students, alumni, and headquarters staff. Standards also should focus on results (for example, membership retention, scholastic achievement, and so on) and recognize the importance of continual improvement strategies.

Concluding Thoughts

"The difficulties some fraternity members create on our campus are substantial, and must be confronted. University administrators and national and international men's and women's fraternity representatives should work in concert to develop a broad range of responses—from taking advantage of 'teaching moments,' to revoking charters" (Foubert, 1995, p. 523). Senior student affairs staff must articulate clearly to all Greek letter organization members, including national and international headquarters and alumni, the institution standards. Campus administrators must emphasize that it is a privilege, not a right, to be on a campus and if chapters do not contribute to the college or university's educational mission and the standards the institution espouses, these organizations will not be welcome. The institution will certainly survive without the Greek organization, but not vice versa. The greatest challenge to the Greek community will be to establish partnerships with college and university administrators and headquarters to address contemporary issues and to develop reasonable expectations through various self-study processes that espouse the high ideals and purposes of Greek letter organizations in the twenty-first century.

References

Anson, J. L., and Marchesani, R. F. (eds.). *Baird's Manual of American College Fraternities.* (20th ed.) Indianapolis, Ind.: Baird's Manual Foundation, 1991.

Council for the Advancement of Standards. *Fraternity and Sorority Advising: Self-Assessment Guide.* College Park: University of Maryland, 1992.

Council for the Advancement of Standards. *Standards and Guidelines for Fraternity and Sorority Advising.* College Park: University of Maryland, 1997.

Foubert, J. D. "A Review of Research on Fraternities: On Balance, They're Worth Having." *Synthesis: Law and Policy in Higher Education,* 1995, 7 (2), 514, 523.

Fraternity Insurance Purchasing Group. "Risk Management Policy." In *Interfraternity Directory.* Indianapolis, Ind.: National Interfraternity Conference, 1996.

Gose, B. "Efforts to End Fraternity Hazing Said to Have Largely Failed: Critics Say State Laws Have Been Ineffective, in Part Because of a Tendency to Blame the Victims." *Chronicle of Higher Education,* Apr. 18, 1997, pp. A37–A38.

Kuh, G. D., Pascarella, E. T., and Wechsler, H. "The Questionable Value of Fraternities." *Chronicle of Higher Education,* 1996, 43 (4), A68.

Lange, D. K. "How to Put the CAS Standards to Work." *AFA Perspectives,* 1986, 23 (7), 1, 4–5.

Mullendore, R. H. "The Joint Statement on Rights and Freedoms of Students, Twenty-Five Years Later." In W. A. Bryan and R. H. Mullendore (eds.), *Rights, Freedoms, and Respon-*

sibilities of Students. New Directions for Student Services, no. 59. San Francisco: Jossey-Bass, 1992.

Mullendore, R. H., and Bryan, W. A. "Rights, Freedoms, and Responsibilities: A Continuing Agenda." In W. A. Bryan and R. H. Mullendore (eds.), *Rights, Freedoms, and Responsibilities of Students.* New Directions for Student Services, no. 59. San Francisco: Jossey-Bass, 1992.

National Association of Student Personnel Administrators. *Reasonable Expectations.* Washington, D.C.: National Association of Student Personnel Administrators, 1996.

Pavela, G. (ed.). "Greek Life: A Foundation for the Future." *Synthesis: Law and Policy in Higher Education,* 1995a, 7 (1), 500, 502, 504–507.

Pavela, G. "Rebuilding the Foundations of Fraternity Life." *Synthesis: Law and Policy in Higher Education,* 1995b, 7 (1), 493.

Pavela, G. "The Power of Association: Defining Our Relationship with Students in the Twenty-First Century." *Synthesis: Law and Policy in Higher Education,* 1996, 7 (3), 529–533, 537–540.

Sigma Alpha Epsilon Fraternity. *Standards Above Excellence.* Evanston, Ill.: Sigma Alpha Epsilon Fraternity, 1996.

MICHAEL D. SHONROCK is dean of students and adjunct assistant professor in the Division of Educational Psychology and Leadership and Department of Higher Education at Texas Tech University.

Senior student affairs officers must thoroughly understand the
challenges facing fraternities and sororities in the twenty-first century.
Using that knowledge, they can employ strategies to address those
challenges and to help students learn, both in and out of the classroom.

Greeks as Communities of Learners

Edward G. Whipple, Eileen G. Sullivan

This volume has made numerous references to *learning community*. It is our belief that if fraternities and sororities want to contribute productively to college and university communities in the next century, they must confront and resolve issues such as those presented in this volume. Why? When they remain unresolved, these issues present barriers to effective learning. For example, a student's failure to learn from others of a different race, ethnicity, or religion does not promote the type of educational outcome institutions seek. Alternatively, if a student has a drinking problem and misses the majority of classes during her semester, how can she be expected to have learned from the instructor or others in the class? Only by aggressively addressing these kinds of challenges can campus administrators hope to help students and faculty develop true learning communities.

The Challenges Facing Greeks Today

This volume has presented important issues about the quality of life in fraternity and sorority chapters. The chapter authors have suggested ways of dealing with significant matters that directly affect Greek life.

Diversity. There is no better time than the present for Greeks to promote and support the richness and importance of campus diversity. It is no secret that historically white fraternities and sororities are soundly criticized for their inability to attract students of color and other underrepresented populations. In the same regard, historically black fraternities and sororities have also been criticized for their unwillingness to diversify their membership. In Chapter Two, Boschini and Thompson wrote that through continued educational efforts, campus administrators must encourage groups to work together for the betterment of the institution and the total learning experience.

NEW DIRECTIONS FOR STUDENT SERVICES, no. 81, Spring 1998 © Jossey-Bass Publishers

Higher education educators and Greek headquarters must join forces to help undergraduate Greeks understand the meaning of diversity and the implications of living in a multicultural world. Fraternity and sorority systems would look and behave much differently if their membership reflected a diversity of skin color, religious affiliation, culture, and ideology. This would, for example, change the kinds of educational programming in which members were interested and social events they desired. In addition, for those fraternity and sorority members living in a house, the residential environment would change. The dynamics of living with someone from a distinctly different religious background or country would change the routines of daily life and the discussion topics at chapter meetings. All of this would contribute to the desired learning outcomes of college.

Critical-Thinking Skills. Both supporters and detractors of Greek life criticize the lack of intellectual life in chapters, in addition to students' inability to think critically. In Chapter Three, Randall and Grady demonstrated that fraternity and sorority members have not made sufficient progress in developing critical thinking. The time that members, pledges, and associate members spend with their chapters can detract from engagement in more educationally purposeful endeavors. In addition, the need to conform to group standards, such as requirements to attend social events, can isolate Greeks from non-Greek peers and from the intellectual and social challenges needed for cognitive development.

Alcohol Use. Greek letter organizations cannot become effective learning communities until they conquer the problem of alcohol abuse and its consequences. Despite institutions' and headquarters' educational efforts and despite policies designed to promote responsible alcohol use, senior student affairs officers continue to be inundated with incidents resulting from Greeks' alcohol abuse. In Chapter Five, Dana and Riordan offered a model and many resources for policies, programs, and strategies that can help institutions and Greeks deal with this extremely serious issue.

The greatest challenge here is the culture of alcohol abuse that exists in both men's and women's Greek organizations. Even institutions that seek to eliminate alcohol from residential chapters must recognize that problem drinking by Greeks occurs in a variety of locations. This reinforces the need for higher education institutions to form coalitions with national and international headquarters; that way, everyone can work together to help fraternities and sororities change their attitudes and behavior.

Legal Issues. It can be argued that the legal concerns that accompany fraternity and sorority activities and behavior pose the greatest threat to Greek letter organizations' relationship with higher education institutions. Thus, these legal issues must be addressed aggressively and responsibly. In Chapter Six, Hennessy and Huson discussed the general liability of institutions that have Greek letter organizations, as well as some specific legal problems. The authors also described an array of potential responses to these legal issues, which senior student affairs officers can consider in collaboration with legal counsel.

Perhaps of greatest concern to institutions are the legal issues surrounding excess drinking and hazing. Hazing—with or without alcohol—is deeply embedded in the cultural system of Greek letter organizations (Kuh, 1996). To realize the educational potential of Greek organizations and to maintain an effective community of learners, higher education institutions must eradicate hazing from the entire fraternity and sorority system. Senior student affairs officers must ensure that their codes of student conduct explicitly say which activities constitute hazing, and they must insist on the most severe penalties for hazing activities. In addition, institutions must provide ongoing educational programs to educate chapter leaders, members, pledges, and associate members about institutional expectations and standards, as well as the dangers and consequences of hazing.

Hazing does not only happen in Greek letter organizations. Widening the hazing discussion to all members of the campus community (for example, athletic teams, music groups) is important. This is not to say that because hazing also occurs in other groups, it lessens the seriousness of its existence in fraternities and sororities. On many campuses, however, the visibility of Greek organizations and activities can give the impression that they are the only organizations that engage in hazing. We recommend that senior student affairs officers and their institutions take a clear "no tolerance" stand on hazing and that the same standards of interpersonal respect are instilled in all student organizations, athletic teams, and campus military groups (for example, ROTC).

Ethical Development. In Chapter Four, Earley highlighted the need for Greek letter organizations to foster ethical development, including decision making, among members. Promoting ethics in the Greek experience means helping fraternity and sorority members become persons of character and integrity, resulting in behavior that supports the institution's educational goals. Ultimately, this means providing members with the skills necessary to narrow the distance between espoused values and actual behavior (Keim, 1991).

Perhaps the words of Martin Luther King, Jr., are applicable as administrators consider the importance of instilling a moral foundation in all: "The function of education . . . is to teach one to think intensively and to think critically. But education which stops with efficiency may prove the greatest menace to society. The most dangerous criminal may be the man gifted with reason but no morals. . . . Intelligence plus character—that is the goal of true education. The complete education gives one not only power of concentration but worthy objectives upon which to concentrate" (Willimon and Naylor, 1995, p. 55).

Senior student affairs officers can help chapters "build character" through education efforts. Greek letter organizations must realize the importance of an institution's educational mission and values. As student affairs staff members work with Greek letter organizations, they must convey the institution's mission and values through their words and actions.

Standards and Expectations. In Chapter Seven, Michael Shonrock pointed to the need for clear, high standards and expectations for fraternities and sororities. Institutions are calling for their Greek systems to prove that they promote experiences consistent with their educational purposes. Senior student affairs officers must work collaboratively and closely with groups that have a vested interest in improving the quality of Greek life. Together, they can establish benchmarks that can help a chapter achieve in areas such as scholarship, service to the institution and community, and responsible behavior. Organizations outside the university community, such as the National Interfraternity Conference, the National Panhellenic Conference, and the National Pan-Hellenic Council, can be included when student affairs officers address standards and expectations for campus Greek systems.

Greek Letter Organizations as Effective Learning Communities

Fraternities and sororities have the potential to create communities that demonstrate, through words and actions, all these positive characteristics. Certainly, in a small, tight-knit group such as a Greek letter organization, members should respect each other, feel comfortable together, and interact with others who may be of a different background. These members should be challenged intellectually by discussions about experiences that have occurred in classrooms and during the day.

Many challenges face Greek letter organizations. Although this *New Directions* volume merely skimmed the surface of current topics related to Greek experiences, one important question recurred during each chapter: Do fraternities and sororities—through their program efforts, individual and group behavior, and relationships with members of the campus community—contribute to the institution's educational mission? Before answering this question, members of Greek letter organizations should first ask questions such as the following:

- Is our fraternity or sorority a learning community? Do our members know what a learning community is? How does our Greek letter organization contribute to the institution's educational mission?
- Do our members understand what *diversity* means? How does our chapter exemplify this meaning on a daily basis? What is the ethnic or racial composition of our chapter?
- Does our chapter educate pledges and members about alcohol abuse? Are older members positive role models for the younger members? Are members held accountable for bad judgment that results in behavior that reflects negatively on our chapter and institution?
- What mechanism is in place to help our pledges or associate members think critically, analyze course material, and make important connections between what is learned in the classroom and what is happening in our chapter? What kinds of programs and experiences do we provide for the development of that critical thinking?
- How do we help students make the "right choice" in life? Is this our obligation? How do ethics and values relate to our chapter? Can we relate a mem-

ber's values to chapter values and ultimately to those of our institution? What does *ethical behavior* mean for a member of a Greek letter organization?
• What standards or expectations for excellence do we have for our chapter? How do these reflect the institution's values? How do we achieve those standards or expectations?

These are the sorts of questions many higher education leaders are asking Greek letter organization members. These same leaders are assessing Greek letter organizations' value to the institution. If fraternities and sororities want to become integral members of the larger campus community, they can no longer afford to provide words without action. They can no longer afford to condone behavior that conflicts with the institution's learning goals. Thus, in response to the question "Do fraternities and sororities contribute to the institution's educational mission?" our answer is "No, not right now."

The follow-up question then becomes "*Can* fraternities and sororities contribute to the institution's educational mission?" Our response to that question is "Yes, if Greek letter organizations understand, confront, and resolve the challenges that face them." If this happens, the result can be the creation of true learning communities that enhance the quality of the student experience.

The Challenge to Change

The first step in creating a learning community is for Greek letter organizations to redefine their priorities and to align those priorities with the educational goals of higher education. Love and Love (1995) have stated that if colleges and universities want learning to occur, "institutions and individuals must put into place actions that correspond with the emerging assumptions regarding the interrelatedness of cognitive, emotional, and social elements of learning. Present cultural norms and practices must be examined and, where appropriate, discarded, while new ones must be nurtured" (p. 43).

Chapter leaders must understand that if the chapter is to be part of the campus community, priorities must change. Ironically, if Greek letter organizations returned to their founding principles and each member practiced those principles daily, their priorities would likely be congruent with the educational mission. Most Greek letter organizations center on principles of sound learning, friendship, service, and rectitude. In some fashion, most institutions' values articulate these same principles.

The second step in creating a learning community is for Greek letter organizations to have strong leaders to initiate and implement change. Forceful, mature student leadership is important for Greek letter organizations. Gabelnick (1997) asserted that the goal of our educating our citizenry is "to prepare new, committed leaders for the 21st century. Yet redesigning general education programs, engaging students in learning communities, fostering community service, and rewarding faculty for action research and community service will only enhance civic virtue and social responsibility if students and teachers begin to see themselves not as actors upon others but as 'new' leaders: partners, facilitators, enablers, and guides" (p. 35).

Not only should administrators and faculty take on new leadership roles but the Greek leadership must also see itself differently. Student leaders of Greek organizations must assume several different roles if they expect change to occur and succeed. They must learn how to be partners, facilitators, enablers, and guides if fraternity and sorority chapters are to confront today's issues successfully.

Greek members may counter that they already are strong leaders on campus. They might state that fraternity and sorority members hold leadership positions in the campus's major student organizations. In addition, these students are also inducted into the top academic honorary societies. They could continue to say that there is probably no greater source of campus and community service than certain Greek letter organizations.

Unfortunately, despite outstanding contributions on the part of some Greek letter organizations, their general inability to confront institutional issues such as those described in this volume affects the very fiber of a college or university. It has resulted most often in members' misbehavior and subsequent bad publicity. This has eroded the many contributions that fraternity and sorority members have made to their institutions and surrounding communities.

Senior student affairs officers must promote aggressive leadership training for students from the freshman to the senior year if change is going to occur. In addition, the institution can provide programs to help alumni work more effectively with fraternities and sororities. This collaboration would be extremely beneficial for undergraduates, as it would allow them to see institutional faculty and staff working with alumni toward common goals. Too often, Greek letter organizations' undergraduate members have attempted to pit their alumni against institution faculty and staff. This usually occurs over issues of institution policies and procedures.

A third step that would help Greek letter organizations create learning communities is member and group involvement on campus. Involvement gives students an opportunity to learn and promotes personal development. For example, students could interact more with faculty, staff, and other students or participate in such activities as student organizations, service learning programs, academic internships, or campus student employment. The Study Group on the Conditions of Excellence in American Higher Education (1984) wrote: "Perhaps the most important [condition] for improving undergraduate education is student involvement. . . . The more time and effort students invest in the learning process and the more intensely they engage in their own education, the greater will be their growth and achievement, their satisfaction with their educational experiences, and their persistence in college, and the more likely they are to continue their learning" (p. 17). To ensure that students have opportunities for involvement, senior student affairs officers can encourage faculty to work collaboratively with students on activities. This will help students make connections between in-class and out-of-class experiences.

The fourth step in creating Greek learning communities is to follow a plan based on sound policies and procedures. Senior student affairs officers can support Greek letter organizations by ensuring that appropriate policies and procedures to help them implement change are developed, implemented, and regularly evaluated. If an institution wants student organizations—including fraternities and sororities—to align themselves more closely with the institution's educational mission and thus to redefine their priorities, the institution must create policies and procedures to help them with this change.

This final step necessitates widespread institutional commitment and involvement. If institutions want Greek letter organizations to redefine their priorities, provide outstanding leadership to the campus community, and have members who contribute to the larger learning community, administrators and faculty must provide guidance, resources, and support for these groups to succeed. It ultimately is the chapter membership's responsibility to change, but student affairs staff can be of valuable assistance.

The senior student affairs officer should have discussions with other key administrative and faculty leadership to develop a clear idea of what role Greeks should play on campus. That role should be articulated to student affairs staff, students, and alumni. They should work together to develop a vision and then an action plan for the future of Greek life on the campus. In developing a Greek learning community that supports the larger campus community, these groups should ask the following questions:

- What is a Greek learning community?
- How does a chapter move from its present philosophy, administration, and programs to those of a learning community?
- How do we educate our members about being part of a learning community?
- How can chapter programming change to reflect the values of the institution?
- What kind of relationship should an institution and Greek letter organization have in a learning community?
- How can a Greek learning community balance the academic, social, and service components?
- What role do faculty members play in a Greek learning community?

If fraternities and sororities commit to redefining their roles and priorities, supporting their leaders, promoting members' involvement on campus, and reworking policies and procedures, they can successfully confront and resolve the issues presented in this volume. Student affairs professionals play a critical role in making this happen. In addition to being "friends" and teachers of Greeks struggling to change their cultures, student affairs staff must firmly hold students accountable for meeting institutional expectations. If the goal is to create learning communities, Greek letter organizations and student affairs staff must share a pervasive commitment to developing environments and experiences that support educational outcomes and to eliminating environments and experiences that inhibit those outcomes. The challenges are great, but we believe that students and their learning are worth the struggle.

References

Gabelnick, F. "Educating a Committed Citizenry." *Change,* Jan.–Feb. 1997, pp. 30–35.

Keim, W. S. *The Education of Character: Lessons for Beginners.* Corvallis, Oreg.: Viaticum Press, 1991.

Kuh, G. D. "Guiding Principles for Creating Seamless Learning Environments for Undergraduates." *Journal of College Student Development,* 1996, 37 (2), 135–148.

Love, P. G., and Love, A. G. "Enhancing Student Learning: Intellectual, Social and Emotional Integration." ASHE-ERIC Higher Education Report no. 4. Washington, D.C.: Association for the Study of Higher Education, 1995.

The Study Group on the Conditions of Excellence in American Higher Education. *Involvement in Learning.* Washington, D.C.: U.S. Department of Education, 1984.

Willimon, W. H., and Naylor, T. H. *The Abandoned Generation: Rethinking Higher Education.* Grand Rapids, Mich.: Eerdmans, 1995.

EDWARD G. WHIPPLE *serves as vice president for student affairs and adjunct associate professor in the Department of Higher Education and Student Affairs at Bowling Green State University in Bowling Green, Ohio. He is a former international president of Phi Delta Theta fraternity.*

EILEEN G. SULLIVAN *is completing her doctoral degree in higher education administration at Bowling Green State University. Prior to attending Bowling Green, she was assistant director of student life for Greek affairs at Eastern Illinois University.*

INDEX

Harvard School of Public Health College Alcohol Study, 50–51

Hayes, M. A., 13

Hazing, 3, 11, 39, 89; alcohol abuse associated with, 50, 51, 68, 69; behaviors constituting, 66–67; institutional policies on, 73; legal cases involving, 64–65, 67; legal issues with, 14, 66–68

Headquarters. *See* Greek headquarters

Healy v. James, 72–73

Heida, D. E., 2, 12, 23

Heim, L. L., 3

Hennessy, N. J., 4, 88

Henry, T., 68, 69

Hodgkinson, H., 19

Holcomb, T., 53, 55

Hope, R. O., 19, 20, 22

Hubbard, S. M., 34

Hughes, M., 15

Hunnicutt, D. M., 55

Huson, L. M., 4, 88

Illinois Wesleyan University, Rabel v., 64

In loco amicis, 46

In loco parentis, 2, 62

Institutions: and diversity, 20–21, 25; liability of, for students' actions, 62–66; policies, of, regulating Greek letter organizations, 51–54, 71–75; standards and expectations of, 80–81

Inter-Association Task Force on Alcohol and Other Substance Abuse Issues, 52

Inter-Association Task Force on Campus Alcohol Issues, 52

Iozzi, L. A., 34, 35

James, Healy v., 72–73

Johnson, C. S., 7

Joint Statement on Rights and Freedoms of Students (Mullendore), 82–83

Jones, B. M., 8

Josephson, M., 39

Kaplin, W. A., 62, 63, 64, 65, 66, 69, 70, 72

Kappa Alpha Society, 8

Kappa Alpha Theta sorority, 8

Karmos, J., 2–3

Keim, M., 2–3

Keim, W. S., 89

Kimbrough, W. M., 3

King, M. L., Jr., 89

King, P. M., 13

Kochis, R., 49

Kohlberg, L., 40, 44, 45

Kramer, R., 40

Kuh, G. D., 2, 9–10, 11, 14, 15, 19, 20, 21, 25, 31, 39, 40, 41, 49, 50, 51, 53, 61, 79, 89

Kurfiss, J. G., 30

Lange, D. K., 82

Leadership training, 43–44, 92

Learning communities, 2; creating, 8–10, 91–94; and diversity, 20; Greek letter organizations as, 15–16, 90–91

Lee, B. A., 62, 63, 64, 65, 66, 69, 70, 72

Legal issues, 4, 14, 61–75, 88–89; with alcohol use/abuse, 14, 53, 68–70; general liability, 62–66; with hazing, 66–68; with sexual assault, 70–71

Lehigh University, Booker v., 74

Leonardi v. Bradley University, 71

Letzring, T. D., 53, 55

Lewis, J., 55

Liability: for actions of students, 62–66; with alcohol abuse, 68–70; with hazing, 66–68; and relationship statements, 72–73; for sexual assaults, 70–71

Liddell, D. L., 45

Linkenbach, J., 42

Loo, C. M., 22

Louisiana State University, 68

Love, A. G., 91

Love, P. G., 91

Lowery, C. R., 45

Lund, J. P., 9, 31

Madrazo-Peterson, R., 22

Maisel, J. P., 11, 15, 39, 61

Manley, R. E., 20

Marchesani, R. F., 1, 12, 15, 79, 81

Marklein, M., 50

Marlowe, A. E., 15

Marshall, S., 69

Martin, P. Y., 15, 39

McCabe, D. L., 39, 43

The Miami Model for Greek Excellence, 80

Miami University, 29, 80

Millard v. Osborne, 65, 73–74

Model Alcohol Policy, 52–53

Ordering Information

NEW DIRECTIONS FOR STUDENT SERVICES is a series of paperback books that offers guidelines and programs for aiding students in their total development—emotional, social, and physical, as well as intellectual. Books in the series are published quarterly in Spring, Summer, Fall, and Winter and are available for purchase by subscription as well as individually.

SUBSCRIPTIONS cost $54.00 for individuals (a savings of 35 percent over single-copy prices) and $90.00 for institutions, agencies, and libraries. Standing orders are accepted. New York residents, add local sales tax for subscriptions. (For subscriptions outside the United States, add $7.00 for shipping via surface mail or $25.00 for air mail. Orders must be prepaid in U.S. dollars by check drawn on a U.S. bank or charged to VISA, MasterCard, or American Express.)

SINGLE COPIES cost $22.00 plus shipping (see below) when payment accompanies order. California, New Jersey, New York, and Washington, D.C., residents, please include appropriate sales tax. Canadian residents, add GST and any local taxes. Billed orders will be charged shipping and handling. No billed shipments to post office boxes. (Orders from outside the United States must be prepaid by check drawn on a U.S. bank or charged to VISA, MasterCard, or American Express.)

SHIPPING (SINGLE COPIES ONLY): $30.00 and under, add $5.50; to $50.00, add $6.50; to $75.00, add $7.50; to $100.00, add $9.00; to $150.00, add $10.00.

ALL PRICES are subject to change.

DISCOUNTS FOR QUANTITY ORDERS are available. Please write to the address below for information.

ALL ORDERS must include either the name of an individual or an official purchase order number. Please submit your order as follows:
   Subscriptions: specify series and year subscription is to begin
   Single copies: include individual title code (such as SS55)

MAIL ALL ORDERS TO:
Jossey-Bass Publishers
350 Sansome Street
San Francisco, California 94104–1342

Phone subscription or single-copy orders toll-free at (888) 378–2537 or at (415) 433–1767 (toll call).
Fax orders toll-free to: (800) 605–2665
FOR SUBSCRIPTION SALES OUTSIDE OF THE UNITED STATES, contact any international subscription agency or Jossey-Bass directly.